# Adam
# SMITH

Available in the Great Thinkers Series

*Thomas Aquinas,* by K. Scott Oliphint
*Francis Bacon,* by David C. Innes
*Karl Barth,* by Shao Kai Tseng
*Richard Dawkins,* by Ransom Poythress
*Gilles Deleuze,* by Christopher Watkin
*Jacques Derrida,* by Christopher Watkin
*Michel Foucault,* by Christopher Watkin
*G. W. F. Hegel,* by Shao Kai Tseng
*David Hume,* by James N. Anderson
*Immanuel Kant,* by Shao Kai Tseng
*Karl Marx,* by William D. Dennison
*Alvin Plantinga,* by Greg Welty
*Plato,* by David Talcott
*Karl Rahner,* by Camden M. Bucey
*Adam Smith,* by Jan van Vliet

"Van Vliet's study of Adam Smith masterfully uncovers this influential progenitor's entire philosophy, from economics to ethics. Flying in the face of caricatures such as laissez-faire and raw capitalism, so often falsely attributed to Smith, this reading reveals how profoundly concerned this philosopher was for the poor and the destitute, as well as other effects of social injustice. At the same time, van Vliet sharply criticizes Smith for his lack of a robust Reformed theological undergirding. The lasting effect of such an honest appraisal of Smith's work is the timeliness of his views, especially in the face of our present cultural upheavals."

—**William Edgar**, Professor of Apologetics Emeritus, Westminster Theological Seminary

"Jan van Vliet has written an excellent work both expositing and summarizing the work of Adam Smith and offering a Reformed Protestant engagement and critique of Smith, with special attention given to the thought of Cornelius Van Til. If you suspect that what you were taught on Adam Smith in your college economics class might be a tad askew, this book is for you. Van Vliet works through the key insights of Smith's *The Theory of Moral Sentiments* and *Wealth of Nations*, and argues persuasively that Smith was concerned with the proper ordering and prospering of the culture as a whole, particularly with justice for the poor and underprivileged. Kudos to van Vliet for a super book."

—**Bradley G. Green**, Professor of Theological Studies, Union University; Visiting Professor of Philosophy and Theology, The Southern Baptist Theological Seminary

"I'm glad to see a volume in the Great Thinkers series on Adam Smith as his influence on contemporary culture is immense. Jan van Vliet gives a compact and helpful summary of Smith's life and main ideas, and his Christian theistic evaluation will I hope provoke more theologians to engage with his work."

—**Paul Oslington**, Professor of Economics and Theology, Alphacrucis University College

# Adam SMITH

Jan van Vliet

P&R
PUBLISHING
P.O. BOX 817 • PHILLIPSBURG • NEW JERSEY 08865-0817

ISBN: 978-1-62995-406-6 (pbk)
ISBN: 978-1-62995-407-3 (ePub)

Printed in the United States of America

**Library of Congress Cataloging-in-Publication Data**

Names: Vliet, Jan van, Ph. D., author.
Title: Adam Smith / Jan van Vliet.
Description: Phillipsburg, New Jersey : P&R Publishing Company, [2024] | Series: Great thinkers | Includes bibliographical references and index. | Summary: "Adam Smith's religion drove his prescriptions for a virtuous humanity and a free and flourishing society. Jan Van Vliet examines how the practical implications of these strike a common chord with Scripture"-- Provided by publisher.
Identifiers: LCCN 2024013357 | ISBN 9781629954066 (paperback) | ISBN 9781629954073 (epub)
Subjects: LCSH: Smith, Adam, 1723-1790. | Philosophers--Scotland--Biography. | Economists--Scotland--Biography.
Classification: LCC B1545.Z7 V55 2024 | DDC 330.15/3092 [B]--dc23/eng/20240603
LC record available at https://lccn.loc.gov/2024013357

For Joan

# CONTENTS

# SERIES INTRODUCTION

Amid the rise and fall of nations and civilizations, the influence of a few great minds has been profound. Some of these remain relatively obscure even as their thought shapes our world; others have become household names. As we engage our cultural and social contexts as ambassadors and witnesses for Christ, we must identify and test against the Word those thinkers who have so singularly formed the present age.

The Great Thinkers series is designed to meet the need for critically assessing the seminal thoughts of these thinkers. Great Thinkers hosts a colorful roster of authors analyzing primary source material against a background of historical contextual issues, and providing rich theological assessment and response from a Reformed perspective.

Each author was invited to meet a threefold goal, so that each Great Thinkers volume is, first, *academically informed*. The brevity of Great Thinkers volumes sets a premium on each author's command of the subject matter and on the secondary discussions that have shaped each thinker's influence. Our authors identify the most influential features of their thinkers' work and address them with precision and insight. Second, the series maintains a high standard of *biblical and theological faithfulness.* Each volume stands on an epistemic commitment to "the whole counsel of God" (Acts 20:27), and is thereby equipped for fruitful critical engagement. Finally, Great Thinkers texts are *accessible,* not burdened with jargon or unnecessarily difficult vocabulary. The goal is to inform and equip the reader as effectively as possible through clear writing, relevant analysis, and incisive, constructive critique. My hope is that this series will distinguish itself by striking with biblical faithfulness and the riches of the Reformed tradition at the central nerves of culture, cultural history, and intellectual heritage.

Bryce Craig, president of P&R Publishing, deserves hearty thanks for his initiative and encouragement in setting the series in motion and seeing it through. Many thanks as well to P&R's director of academic development, John Hughes, who has assumed, with cool efficiency, nearly every role on the production side of each volume. The Rev. Mark Moser carried much of the burden in the initial design of the series, acquisitions, and editing of the first several volumes. And the expert participation of Amanda Martin, P&R's editorial director, was essential at every turn. I have long admired P&R Publishing's commitment, steadfast now for over eighty-five years, to publishing excellent books promoting biblical understanding and cultural awareness, especially in the area of Christian apologetics. Sincere thanks to P&R, to these fine brothers and sisters, and to several others not mentioned here for the opportunity to serve as editor of the Great Thinkers series.

Nathan D. Shannon
Seoul, Korea

# FOREWORD

Like most other students of Adam Smith, my initial attraction was based on prima facie commitments to classical economics. Smith's *Wealth of Nations* was a known tour de force in making the case for rational self-interest, free trade and free exchange, division of labor, and other accepted cornerstones of a free-enterprise system. And like most other students of Adam Smith who have an interest in ethics and philosophy, my economic attraction soon expanded into the arena of moral philosophy, where *Theory of Moral Sentiments* became a powerful supplement—a prequel, if you will—to the classical economic argument in *Wealth of Nations*. This handy one-two punch became, and remains, a more holistic appeal in a believer's advocacy of a market economy. In Smith, one finds support for the free *and* virtuous society.

Yet my intellectual and personal interest in Adam Smith would expand even beyond the robustness of his harmonized presentation of human flourishing. Contemporary scholars can be expected to appeal to particular figures of history who align with their own argument in a given field or discipline. Indeed, the great thinkers of history own the shoulders that contemporaries stand on. But with Smith, my own expanded study of economics over the years revealed something that was not previously known to me: many different contemporaries of many different schools of thought and economic or social orientation were claiming him as their own. *This*, in and of itself, became fascinating to me, warranting expanded inquiry.

Free marketeers do not often appeal to Karl Marx to make their case. Collectivists do not generally appeal to Ludwig von Mises to make their case. Hedonists do not cite the apostle Paul or Friedrich Nietzsche. Leading proponents of various schools of thought may reference their ideological nemesis, but they do not claim their opposition as a basis for support of their argument. But when it came to Adam Smith, there seemed to be a plethora of exceptions to this. Either Smith was the most intellectually schizophrenic scholar of the last four hundred years or a vast and even systemic effort was underway to *rewrite* Smith so as to make him one of their own. Were this many economists and policymakers really this dishonest, agendized, or confused? Or was there something in the life and work of Adam Smith that attracted revisionism? Understanding the pieces of this puzzle became a subject of intense study in my own scholarly pursuits.

What one discovers in a rigorous analysis of Adam Smith, such as this very work by Jan van Vliet, is the Adam Smith that you thought you understood him to be—an ethicist who was in many ways a product of his philosophical time. The influence of David Hume and the Scottish Enlightenment looms large. In the evolution of classical economics, it was Smith who would influence other leading figures of the decades that followed (from Ricardo to Say). The full-orbed doctrines in Smith's seminal works were irresistible in the modern formation of a market economy rooted to a coherent understanding of social cooperation. This study by van Vliet is indispensable in upholding Smith as he was, and indeed as we thought him to be: a defender of a moral economy rooted in the dual reality of human aspiration and human sympathy.

So why does Smith hold such a unique ability to attract adherents to competing systems of thought to claim him as their own? Is it just that Smith provides "ornaments" for lazy, dishonest, tired, and distorted agendas? I have come to discover that there is a unique desire, and even scholarly need, for us all to have "our own Adam Smith." Secularized and humanistic proponents of consumerism want intellectual and moral bona fides to appeal to, and Smith provides them the fodder from which they can then execute sweeping distortion of his actual views. Social-justice proponents, for whom Smith's anti-mercantilism and embedded commitment to freedom of exchange would be anathema, find for themselves just enough rhetorical device to use Smith in their own "ornamental" fashion. Yet it is not just laziness but actual dishonesty that would allow Smith to be used this way in contemporary debate—as a tool for either materialists or welfare-statists, depending on one's own presuppositional commitments. Smith has become not a debate about his actual beliefs, but a debate about *our beliefs*, under the revisionist guise that we are "unpacking" what he actually proposed.

This is why Adam Smith is so important—and why this work is so valuable. Coherently harmonizing moral philosophy and political economy remains the profound debate of our "contemporaneous reality." Our own political debate, economic divide, and philosophical division center on an embedded tension that Smith was addressing two and a half centuries ago. Smith is revised and distorted by those looking for a theoretical support that has stood the test of time for contemporary formulations that are flawed, internally contradicted, and unable to satisfy the conditions of human flourishing.

What an honest read and analysis of Adam Smith will provide is a "vision of a prosperous, free, and flourishing society, embedded in traditional moral values." What it will not provide is a view of man as the "ultimate atom with measurable desires." The need of the hour for Christians devoted to the free and virtuous society is a deeper and more robust reconciliation of mankind as made in the image of God, with tremendous capacity in our pursuit of enlightened self-interest, who also carries moral responsibility as an economic actor and member of various human communities.

A fully Reformed and Christian approach to this need of the hour will inevitably vary from certain metaphysical and epistemological commitments of Adam Smith. His Enlightenment-era deficiencies are unavoidable and unsurprising. But a Reformed and Christian social theory of markets that promotes freedom and virtue will stand on the shoulders of Adam Smith. This work is a giant bridge toward that needed understanding.

David L. Bahnsen
Managing Partner and Chief Investment Officer,
The Bahnsen Group

# PREFACE

I am writing this preface with one eye trained on a yellowed and frazzled eight-page, narrow-ruled, handwritten book report dated May 1974. The subject is Adam Smith's *Wealth of Nations* (the Penguin edition of 1970, edited by Andrew Skinner and containing Books 1–3), a topic I had chosen for my Grade 13 history project upon my return to high school after a four-year hiatus. Thus, I have known and worked with Adam Smith, in varying degrees of intensity, for exactly half a century.

As I consider this rather lengthy inquiry, certain things stand out. Smith and his corpus are massively impressive, a veritable edifice of social theory, philosophy, and political economy, mingled with political science, history, economics, anthropology, and sociology, all working together to create a theory of human interaction, social history, and the building of a virtuous society. My focus has been on his *magna opera,* but he was a polymath of the highest order. Interpreting Smith has been, for me, a group project, gathering together the collected wisdom and insight of phenomenal Smithian scholars, who have proven to be both accessible and, when contacted in real time, highly approachable and generous with their time. The analytical acuity and personal humility of these scholars, past and present, has been an inspiration for me, always pushing me higher and harder to get Smith right.

For the perspectival contribution of this volume, I am similarly indebted. The reader will notice the interpretative principles of covenantal apologetics, epistemology, and ethics, applied throughout. Further, the wealth of the neo-Calvinist tradition has also been brought to bear on the perspectival evaluation of Adam Smith, particularly in the area of human flourishing.

I am deeply indebted to the editorial team of P&R Publishing —in particular, Nathan Shannon, James Scott, and John Hughes— who have always pushed for clarity and improvement. Your patience and gentle but firm nudging are deeply appreciated and have vastly improved the final product.

My institution, Dordt University, has been generous in the provision of time and space to develop the project. My teaching assistants over the years—in particular Olivia (Couch) Arkema, who, as my summer research assistant, summarized all the chapters in both *Theory of Moral Sentiments* and *Wealth of Nations*— have granted me space to pursue this project among my other institutional responsibilities. And the library staff, under the able leadership of Jenni Breems, was indispensable in chasing down references, particularly the most obscure ones. Not once over the years, particularly during the finishing stages of the writing project, did they come up empty-handed.

Friends near and far proved indispensable from start to finish. The research and writing had its origins a few years ago within the wonderful serenity of a spacious condominium in the Canadian subarctic—Yellowknife, Canada—from whence I watched the ice breaking up on the shores of Great Slave Lake in late May and early June. Interestingly, the last part of the formal writing took place in Yellowknife as well, in the darkness of winter. My deepest appreciation goes to our good friends David and Hilda Weaver for provision of this contemplative space.

A much greater event to come out of my return to high school —greater even than meeting Adam Smith—was the meeting of a teenage girl named Joan, who became my long-suffering wife and the mother of my children. This project would not have concluded without her support of my scholarly inclinations, her encouragement, her tolerance of my absentmindedness, and her occasional but necessary prodding. It is to her that this book is joyfully dedicated.

# ABBREVIATIONS OF SMITH'S WORKS

All references to the Adam Smith corpus are to the Glasgow Edition, published in hardcover by Oxford University Press and in paperback by Liberty Fund in Indianapolis, IN. Text references and citations are by page number rather than the more conventional system of subdivisions.

| | |
|---|---|
| *Corr.* | *Correspondence of Adam Smith*, ed. E. C. Mossner and I. S. Ross (1987) |
| *EPS* | *Essays on Philosophical Subjects*, ed. W. P. D. Wightman, J. C. Bryce, and I. S. Ross (1982) |
| *HA* | *The Principles which lead and direct Philosophical Enquiries illustrated by the History of Astronomy*, in *EPS* |
| *LJ* | *Lectures on Jurisprudence*, ed. R. L. Meek, D. D. Raphael, and P. G. Stein (1982) |
| *LJ(A)* | *Lectures on Jurisprudence* (1762–63) |
| *LJ(B)* | *Lectures on Jurisprudence* (1766) |

*LRBL* *Lectures on Rhetoric and Belles Lettres*, ed. J. C. Bryce (1985)

*TMS* *The Theory of Moral Sentiments*, ed. D. D. Raphael and A. L. Macfie (1982)

*WN* *An Inquiry into the Nature and Causes of the Wealth of Nations*, ed. R. H. Campbell and A. S. Skinner (1981)

# 1

# INTRODUCTION

## Historical Moments

The year 2023 marked the tercentenary of the birth of Adam Smith (1723–90). Smith ranks among the greatest intellectuals of his age. As a key representative of the Scottish Enlightenment, he cast a long shadow, both during his lifetime and beyond. Two and a quarter centuries after his life and contemporary influence, he and his corpus continue to be labeled, mislabeled, examined, reexamined, studied, interpreted, claimed, reclaimed, disclaimed, challenged, applied, and misapplied. Smith's thought constitutes a perpetual presence in the consciousness of all who pay even superficial attention to contemporary socioeconomic life and thought. He was a renaissance man who encouraged the development of early modern Europe in, among other areas, science, philosophy, and culture.

Considering briefly the momentous time in history when Smith appeared on the world stage will bring us some distance to understanding the historical momentum that contributed to the tremendous significance of the man and his work.

The Scottish Enlightenment with all its associated achievements—particularly in the realm of the intellect—was under way.

Empiricism and skepticism ruled the day; Descartes (1596–1650) had receded into the background. A new dawn of profound intellectual endeavor had broken in the most unlikely of places: the relative backwater of eighteenth-century Scotland. Luminous individuals, such as David Hume (1711–76, philosophy), James Hutton (1726–97, geology), Thomas Reid (1710–96, philosophy), Francis Hutcheson (1694–1746, philosophy), and Adam Ferguson (1723–1816, philosophy and history), together both inhabited and constructed this rarefied world of enlightenment, science, and progress, of which today, almost a quarter of a millennium later, we continue to be the beneficiaries. Adam Smith certainly did his part in moral philosophy, political philosophy, political economy, economic science, history, rhetoric, agriculture—and the list is far from exhausted, as we shall see throughout the following account. Taken together, inhabitants of that world exerted a most disproportionate influence on modernity.

The French Revolution and its reverberations throughout Europe and then the rest of the world came on the very cusp of our Smithian period. The Bastille was stormed one year less three days before the death of Adam Smith, and little is known of his personal views regarding this epoch-making event, although much has been speculated about the impact of his work on post-revolutionary France.[1]

Whether or not—and, if so, to what degree—Adam Smith engaged the Industrial Revolution in Scotland remains a matter of scholarly dispute. This debate can be settled with some degree of confidence only when agreement is reached on the genesis of the revolution in Scotland—a consensus which has proven to be notoriously elusive. Variance of only a few years in dating that event may result in including the period when Smith was active

1. See, for example, Richard Whatmore, "Adam Smith's Role in the French Revolution," *Past and Present* 175 (May 2002): 65–89.

or excluding it entirely. About one predication there can be little doubt: processes prescribed and described in Smith's work on political economy were already in play in industrial Europe. But association does not imply causality. Claims that Adam Smith was capitalism's "earliest interpreter" or "the philosopher of the capitalist revolution" were dismissed out of hand decades ago by Richard Koebner, who asserted that "an attempt to determine Adam Smith's attitude toward the Industrial Revolution might appear to be question-begging."[2] A search of *WN* for references to then contemporary developments in industrial technique and business organization turns out to be a fruitless pursuit. Smith had plenty of opportunity, notably between the years 1767 and 1775, to pay attention to these matters, but he didn't.[3]

That is why it is somewhat surprising that Smith engaged issues associated with the American Revolution with such gusto. That historical moment—generally dated from roughly 1765 to 1783—and the economic system that lay at the heart of the colonial uprising constitute an entire chapter in *WN*.[4] It is a historical coincidence of the highest order that his far-reaching and classic *WN* was published only four months before the Continental Congress adopted the Declaration of Independence authored by Smith's kindred spirits John Adams, Benjamin Franklin, Thomas Jefferson, Roger Sherman, and Robert Livingston, even if Jefferson was the primary author.[5]

2. Richard Koebner, "Adam Smith and the Industrial Revolution," *The Economic History Review* 11, no. 3 (1959): 381–91.

3. Koebner, "Industrial Revolution," 382–83.

4. *WN*, 556–641.

5. I would be remiss to conclude this section on Smith's relationship to these historical developments, particularly the Enlightenment, without drawing attention to some compelling, if sometimes provocative, hypotheses presented in an excellent essay on "Adam Smith and Enlightenment Studies" by Fredrik Albritton Jonsson in *Adam Smith: His Life, Thought, and Legacy*, ed. Ryan Patrick Hanley (Princeton: Princeton University Press, 2016), 443–58.

## Contemporary Considerations

Smith's thought and influence continue to reach across time and space. Contemporary learned and informed debate on political economy, role of government, economic policy recommendations, the interrelatedness and interdependence of humanity, and more, often resounds with his prescriptive and authoritative voice. He has a permanent seat in the public square.

A recent issue of *The Economist* carried an article on the perennial coexistence of both very rich and desperately impoverished nations. It was observed that the earliest economists studied this phenomenon and gave it cultural explanations. It was further asserted that Adam Smith in particular showed a concern for economic development, as is clear from the very title of his famous 1776 work, *An Inquiry into the Nature and Causes of the Wealth of Nations*. These concerns centered on the beliefs, preferences, and values of a society. Does culture help or hinder capitalism? How do the cultures of rich and poor nations compare? What are the norms by which a market economy thrives? The magazine faithfully interpreted the central Smithian premise—so often misinterpreted, misunderstood, and thus misrepresented—that "people would be self-interested, but that they would satisfy their self-interest by adapting to the needs of others."[6] Here we see Smith's focus on the significance of social capital in moving economies forward. Even if the twenty-first century global economy is more complicated than was Smith's point of reference, this central Smithian premise is a good place to start.

The relativism, moral decay, loss of foundational truth, and fractious public discourse characterizing twenty-first century democracies would benefit from attending to Adam Smith's discourse on virtue, comprised of a sense of common humanity, justice, generosity, and public spirit. The enormous injustice

6. "Hard Work and Black Swans," *The Economist*, September 5, 2020, 57.

foisted upon, above all, the trusting aged and pensioned and the perfect storm of events that brought about the Great Recession of 2007–9 and the human carnage that ensued bring to mind the need to return to a caring humanity. Smith was highly suspicious of powerful economic interests, such as monopolies. The various dimensions of the Great Recession—the poor judgment driving bankers' issuance of subprime mortgages, the unmitigated greed behind the failures of the investment houses and banks (and the subsequent bailouts with public money), the ever-increasing housing prices based on artificially high values, and the associated insatiable appetite for material goods—all underscore a human nature playing fast and loose with historically honored principles of morality and ethics. It is time to be reminded of a moral code, and reading Smith is extremely helpful in that regard.

The world is still emerging from the throes of what has been judged to be the first pandemic (Covid-19) since the Spanish flu of 1918. The human toll has been tremendous—millions of lives lost worldwide, the associated decimation of economies and government finances, and the social and personal costs of mandated social isolation and distancing. Humans are social creatures, and Adam Smith has much to say about the interrelatedness and social interactions of all humanity, created to be interdependent.

Finally, the sheer volume and scope of the secondary literature on Adam Smith demands attention. *The Oxford Handbook of Adam Smith*[7] and *The Cambridge Companion to Adam Smith*[8] are both exhaustive tomes in their own right, more encyclopedic than quick reference guides. These two volumes alone demonstrate that Smith is not constrained by time, space, or interpretive philosophy. He still today insists to be read.

7. Christopher J. Berry, Maria Pia Paganelli, and Craig Smith, eds., *The Oxford Handbook of Adam Smith* (Oxford: Oxford University Press, 2013).

8. Knud Haakonssen, ed., *The Cambridge Companion to Adam Smith* (Cambridge: Cambridge University Press, 2006).

## Smithian Hermeneutics

It is generally acknowledged by Smithian scholars that for the first two centuries or so after the publication of *The Wealth of Nations* (*WN*), a regular item on the menu of Smithian scholarship was what came to be known as the Adam Smith Problem (ASP), that is, the apparent contradiction between his formal writing on moral theory and that on political economy. The opening thesis of the former work, *The Theory of Moral Sentiments* (*TMS*) states that human motivation and action are very much influenced—if not dominated—by considerations of the well-being of one's neighbor, while the central principle of the latter is that economic endeavor and optimal economic development are driven by the unambiguous pursuit of self-interest. Is there an earlier and a later Smith, as there are with so many historic individuals with voluminous literary output? What explains this demonstrable lack of inner coherence in what are commonly considered the *magna opera* of a key Enlightenment thinker? The problem apparently does not lie with Adam Smith, but rather with his interpreters, since few today believe that he postulates two contradictory principles of human action. This thesis loses some force when we realize that over the course of his life, Smith was continually engaged with his moral theory—considering its many editions and redactions—even in the penning of his political economy. Further, the discovery in 1958 of two sets of student notes on rhetoric and jurisprudence gave significant clarity to Smithian interpretation and provided a much-needed link in bridging the perceived discontinuity between *TMS* and *WN*. With this the ASP dissipated around the time of the republication, in 1976, of the highly acclaimed "Glasgow Edition" of his work and correspondence. This new edition of the Smithian corpus, timed to appear on the bicentenary of the release of his major work on political economy, both renewed interest in Adam Smith and democratized his work by making it more accessible.

Paradoxically, even though Smith is now more accessible, he is not necessarily more read outside the scholarly world. While many claim to be Smithian experts, it is probably more accurate to say that there is only a vague familiarity with him—or, as one biographer put it, a "popular awareness." A typical essay in the secondary literature on Smith and his thought, or his influence or legacy, opens these days with the cliché that "many quote Adam Smith while very few have read him." In his inimitable way, economist John Kenneth Galbraith gets at the heart of this issue when commenting on Smith's appeal in the pro-capitalist, antigovernment circles of the Reagan administration. In their opposition to government involvement in areas "not in the service of contentment . . . the presidential acolytes in Mr. Reagan's White House wore neckties bearing the picture of the master," even while crassly misrepresenting Smith's thought. "It is perhaps unfortunate that few, perhaps none, who so cited Adam Smith had read his great work," says Galbraith.[9]

But worse than being not read is being misread. Smith is often unfairly and poorly represented because of partial readings and selective and hasty interpretations driving agenda-promoting claims. Unbridled, no-nonsense capitalism, for example, is often advanced in the discourse of political economy and imbued with the vested authority of the Smithian imprimatur. In promotion of such unbounded capitalism, the most egregious abuses of Smith can be seen to fall into at least three related categories: that the market economy is self-regulating, that the profit motive drives rational behavior, and that self-interest alone guarantees "socially productive behavior."[10] These are not Smithian doctrines.

Preeminent Smithian scholar Andrew Skinner did much to consolidate Adam Smith's place in intellectual history by rightly

9. John Kenneth Galbraith, *The Culture of Contentment* (Boston: Houghton Mifflin, 1992), 98–101.

10. Amartya Sen, "Uses and Abuses of Adam Smith," *History of Political Economy* 43 (2011): 257–71.

interpreting him as a system builder who employed the unique approach to social science then current in the philosophical milieu of the Scottish Enlightenment.[11] This method is empirical-historical and is seen particularly in *WN*. The result of this methodology is a neat, logical, and systematic assembly of the system's component parts within the broader historical and institutional features of *WN*. Smith's expertise lies in the philosophical, historical, and economic realms—and each of these dimensions appears distinctly as a crucial component of the whole. To obtain the full force of Smith's project and to optimize its intelligibility, this system must be considered both in its systematic entirety and in its component parts—the three dimensions of Smith's political economy.

This entire project is constructed on the foundation of *TMS* with key teachings from *Lectures on Jurisprudence* (*LJ*). We now see that Smith composed the model of a commercial society progressing through four stages of socioeconomic systems. This society represents a social system facilitated by the principles of human nature—the psychological attributes—observed and explained by Smith in *WN*. Again, in line with the philosophical and epistemological tenets of the Scottish Enlightenment, this entire process of social development was understood and communicated deductively. Thus seen, his political economy should be considered as only part of his comprehensive philosophical system centering on the nature of human behavior.

The narrative that unfolds in the present study incorporates these ingredients, some of which receive more focused attention and elaboration. It will become evident that Smith's life and thought represent a world order shifting into modernity. As Smith scholar James Buchan has written:

11. Jeffrey T. Young, "Andrew Skinner, the Glasgow Edition, and Adam Smith," *Œconomia* 2–3 (2012): 365–76.

> Smith stands at the point where history changes direction. During his lifetime . . . the failed kingdom of drink, the Bible, and the dagger that was old Scotland became a pioneer of the new sciences. God was dismissed from the lecture hall and the drawing room. The old medieval departments of learning disintegrated. Psychology became a study not of the soul but of the passions. Political economy was separated out of moral philosophy and began its progress to respectability and then hegemony. Smith was at the heart of these changes.[12]

12. James Buchan, "The Biography of Adam Smith," in *Adam Smith: His Life*, ed. Hanley, 3.

# 2

# A LIFE IN THE ENLIGHTENMENT WORLD OF MORAL PHILOSOPHY AND THE OLD ECONOMIC ORDER

All great individuals throughout history, regardless of discipline, appear to provide a well-stocked cache of fodder for the biographer.[1] In fact, it is often the case that stories need to be told and retold as newly discovered snippets of information enter the biographer's

1. This account uses multiple biographies of Adam Smith, from his earliest "memorialist" to more recent renditions. The chief sources used are Dugald Stewart, *Account of the Life and Writings of Adam Smith, LL.D.* (1793), in *EPS*, 269–351; John Rae, *Life of Adam Smith* (London: Macmillan, 1895); Jerry Z. Muller, *Adam Smith in His Time and Ours: Designing the Decent Society* (Princeton, NJ: Princeton University Press, 1995), 15–27; Ian Simpson Ross, *The Life of Adam Smith* (Oxford: Oxford University Press, 1995); Christopher J. Berry, "Adam Smith: An Outline of Life, Times, and Legacy," in *The Oxford Handbook of Adam Smith*, ed. Christopher J. Berry, Maria Pia Paganelli, and Craig Smith (Oxford: Oxford University Press, 2013), 1–20; James Buchan, "The Biography of Adam Smith," in *Adam Smith: His Life, Thought, and Legacy*, ed. Ryan Patrick Hanley (Princeton, NJ: Princeton University Press, 2016), 3–16; Jack Russell Weinstein, "Adam Smith (1723–90)," *Internet Encyclopedia of Philosophy*, https://iep.utm.edu/smith/.

realm. It is no different with Adam Smith. It seems as if the further removed in time, the greater the need to recount his life and times. The biographical field of vision this has given rise to over a quarter of a millennium has itself engendered a significant body of literature, the sight lines through which are not always clear. Even if clarity is sometimes lacking, however, the reading of these multiple narratives is a fruitful and often entertaining pursuit—certainly a more agreeable exercise than that provided by a mere encyclopedia entry. Although the following biography has combed the sometimes uneven landscape of a multitude of chroniclers, it presents the consensus view, as it were, of a life well lived. It must be noted that all biographies can be traced back, in varying degrees, to Smith's earliest memorialist, Dugald Stewart (1753–1828), a member of Smith's inner circle who had at one point declared, "I hate biography," yet did a stellar, if somewhat hagiographical, job recounting the life and work of his friend in two readings before the Royal Society of Edinburgh during the winter of 1793.

Some chroniclers opine that this life appears to offer "small incident" to the biographer. It was a rather plain life, it appears, for an individual who is a "household name" and "one of the brightest ornaments of the literature of Scotland." The person regarded by Voltaire as a "great" and "incomparable man" (while bemoaning France's lack of an individual of comparable stature) never penned an autobiography and was a poor correspondent.[2] In this regard, he stands in bold relief over against his close friend David Hume, who supplied an ample amount of both.

## Early Life and Education

Adam Smith was born in 1723 in the port town of Kirkaldy, on the east coast of Scotland, to a recently widowed but well-to-do

2. Robert Chambers and Thomas Napier Thomson, *A Biographical Dictionary of Eminent Scotsmen* (Glasgow: Blackie and Son, 1857), 7:278.

Calvinist, a doting mother who predeceased him by only six years and with whom he remained close his entire life. He was baptized on June 23 into the Church of Scotland, and that date doubles as his birth date, which is unknown. Following homeschooling by tutors, he attended the local grammar school, demonstrating aptitude in memory, academics (especially Latin, math, history, and writing), and talking to himself, even in company. His habits of absentmindedness were also formed early, but he fell short in athletic prowess and similar student activities due to a weak constitution. Smith also learned that the ruling presbyteries could do nothing about the school's stage plays, toward which they exhibited their typical dislike, overruled as they were by a town that supported these plays in both spirit and finance. Smith's kindness, even-mindedness, and generosity also stood out. All these essentials of Smith's character, early education, and formative life lessons consistently evidenced themselves in multiple ways throughout the span of his life.

The University of Glasgow happily accepted the matriculation of Adam Smith at age 14, as well as the stipend that supported him. This was not an entirely uncommon rate of academic progression at the time. Already armed with four years of classics, he engaged in mathematics and natural philosophy, but it was moral philosophy and political history—"the study of human nature in all its branches"—that created in Smith an enduring interest in the improvement of humanity. And while he was exposed to a number of impressive teachers under whom he honed his competencies in mathematics and Greek, among other things, it was moral philosophy that swept him off his feet, particularly as taught by one of the founding fathers of the Enlightenment in Scotland, Francis Hutcheson.[3] It was to this inspiring individual that Smith owed

3. See William R. Scott, "The Never to Be Forgotten Hutcheson: Excerpts from W. R. Scott," *Economic Journal Watch* 8, no. 1 (2011): 96–109; Phyllis Vandenberg and Abigail DeHart, "Francis Hutcheson," *Internet Encyclopedia of Philosophy*, https://iep.utm.edu/hutcheso/.

much of his own subsequent thought; it was also Hutcheson, as one of the leaders of the new philosophical movement, who would receive censure from many orthodox Presbyterians.[4]

## The Emerging "Moral Sense" in Moral Philosophy

Born in Ireland to a Presbyterian minister, Hutcheson left an indelible influence upon his students in both the form and content of his teaching. He was the first at Glasgow to teach in English rather than Latin and did so in a lively, memorable style—a characteristic, it was commonly held, not found in his writings. His oratorical fervor came from his preaching. While a Presbyterian minister himself, he often overstepped the boundary between revelation and reason in his lecture material. For such teaching and for violating his own subscription to the Westminster Confession, he came under censure from the old ecclesiastical order; from his students, on the other hand, he received rave reviews. Many of them would become famous in their own right, not the least of whom was Adam Smith. Half a century later, in the latter stage of his life, Smith expressed deep appreciation for his time at Glasgow and for a teacher of such stature. He mentioned Hutcheson by name.

Hutcheson's theological and philosophical commitments were more deistic than Presbyterian, and he faithfully promulgated its central tenets, one of which was that God was in the business of revealing himself through science and reason, rather than something as opaque as revelation, mystery, and providence. In the area of epistemology, he held that God was known through evidence of his actions in history to ensure "the greatest happiness of the

4. Some of the censure came in a satirical vein from, for example, John Witherspoon (1723–94), fifteen years prior to his passage to New Jersey to take up the presidency of the College of New Jersey (now Princeton University), who was a signer of the U.S. Declaration of Independence (Alasdair MacIntyre, *Whose Justice? Which Rationality?* [South Bend, IN: University of Notre Dame Press, 1988], 244).

greatest number."[5] He maintained that one's knowledge of good and evil was obtainable without reference to the knowledge of God in general revelation. Central to his system of ethics was the principle that the promotion of others' happiness comprised the standard of moral goodness, again absent of any reference to general or special revelation. Hutcheson was an early architect of the Moral Sense school of philosophy.[6]

This folded in well with the developing Scottish moral philosophy of the eighteenth century in both explaining and refining the conviction that human altruism and benevolence were determined without appeal to revelation. Hutcheson opposed the prevailing explanation that self-interest, even egoism practiced through the exercise of "private vices," had socially beneficial consequences. Both Bernard Mandeville (1670–1733) and before him Thomas Hobbes (1588–1679) had made this argument.

While lecturing on his theories of human nature, and with Smith listening closely, Hutcheson made the case for a divinely implanted "moral sense," an innate capacity of humanity to delight in benevolent behavior. This anthropological reality, taught Hutcheson, supplies the psychological basis for virtue. In keeping with the intellectual zeitgeist, particularly the empirical aesthetics of the day, Hutcheson's program of moral philosophy was largely

5. According to biographer Rae, Hutcheson coined this phrase familiar to utilitarians.

6. Hutcheson built on the work of Lord Shaftesbury (1671–1713); together these are considered the chief founders of the Moral Sense school of philosophy. Shaftesbury maintained that "humans are designed to appreciate order and harmony, and that proper appreciation of order and harmony is the basis of correct judgments about morality, beauty, and religion. He was at the forefront of developing the idea of a moral sense, of explicating aesthetic experience, of defending political liberty and tolerance, and of arguing for religious belief based on reason and observation rather than revelation or scripture. Shaftesbury thought the purpose of philosophy was to help enable people to live better lives." Michael B. Gill, "Lord Shaftesbury [Anthony Ashley Cooper, 3rd Earl of Shaftesbury]," in *Stanford Encyclopedia of Philosophy Archive* (Winter 2017 Edition), https://plato.stanford.edu/archives/win2017/entries/shaftesbury/.

empirical in nature, although reason did play a vital role in informing the moral sense. Hutcheson held that while one is instinctually driven by nature to desire the well-being of others, and this desire influences our moral sense of approval or disapproval of an action, the function of reason is to join with the intellect in pursuit of that salutary goal. Reason does not motivate or judge. Reason informs the moral sense and supplies it with content—for example, what is good for others and the greater public good. It is the job of the volitions to desire the chief good, that being the welfare of others.[7]

Thus, the moral sense is the faculty with which the value of an action is felt; it is not the basis of moral decisions or the justification of our approval or disapproval. It is the faculty by which we assess something as morally good or not; it is thus an evaluative faculty. When an agent or a spectator reflects on an action in reference to its circumstances, the moral sense is called into play, particularly when observing the action's consequences for others. This is the ultimate criterion by which our moral senses are exercised.

While Hutcheson wrote no treatise on political economy, many of Smith's developed ideas had their genesis in the philosopher's classroom. In his classes on jurisprudence and his lectures on the state, Hutcheson commented on such economic concepts as labor, value, money, and private ownership within the broader framework of the nature and growth of commerce. Smith heard these lectures and reworked many of Hutcheson's embryonic ideas into a fully developed and refined system in *TMS* and *WN*.

## Later Formal Schooling

Studying at Glasgow for only three years, instead of the requisite four, did not entitle him to a degree, but Adam Smith's real

7. Hutcheson is using Aristotle here (for whom this *summum bonum* was a particular form of happiness).

academic goal was Oxford anyway. Glasgow had merely been a three-year pause on the way to England—by horseback, as it turned out. Once there, it was nothing like he had expected; he was sorely disappointed in the atmosphere at Oxford and would later characterize it and other ancient, rich, and well-endowed universities as "sanctuaries in which exploded systems and obsolete prejudices found shelter and protection, after they had been hunted out of every other corner of the world," and where tenure explained professors' negligence.[8] Coming shortly after Smith, historian Edward Gibbon (1737–94)[9] complained that in place of scholarship, the school majored in administrative chatter, Tory politics, personal anecdotes, and gossip. We can posit that Smith's reverence for Hutcheson, referred to in his correspondence as "the never to be forgotten Hutcheson,"[10] may in part explain his disdain for Oxford. Only David Hume received the same accolade in a laudatory letter that Smith wrote upon Hume's death.[11] These two "never to be forgottens" are generally thought to have been the two greatest influences on Smith.[12]

But Smith redeemed the time there well, staying for fully six years until 1746, despite a perceptible anti-Scottish bias, little social intercourse of any form, close watch over his literary appetites—which resulted in admonishment for the reading of Hume's *Treatise of Human Nature*—and continuing complaints about his health and inclination to laziness, as he shared in letters to his mother. Quite fortuitously, however, the environment created by this arrangement, and ready access to the intellectual resources found in the rich library system, provided Smith the requisite time

8. *WN*, 772.

9. Another well-known contemporary and historian, who famously penned the six-volume *The History of the Decline and Fall of the Roman Empire* between 1776 and 1788.

10. *Corr.*, 308–9.

11. *Corr.*, 220.

12. Scott, "Never to Be Forgotten Hutcheson," 97.

and space to nourish his expansive, cross-disciplinary intellectual appetite. He indulged not only the Greek and Latin classics, but also Italian poetry and French and English literature and, of course, philosophy. His predilection for mathematics and science received further nurture; he revered Newton.

## From Edinburgh Lectures to Glasgow

The strings attached to the bursary on which he attended Oxford led many to believe that Smith was destined to an ecclesiastical life in the Church of England, but, unwilling to commit to such a future, Smith spent two years with his mother in Kirkcaldy, from 1746 to 1748. Through his connections, Smith landed an invitation to deliver a set of lectures primarily on rhetoric and probably also belles lettres and jurisprudence at the capital of Edinburgh. It cannot be said with certainty that these lectures received significant revision when delivered in Glasgow in 1762–63, but the content of these Edinburgh lectures bears close relationship to the student notes discovered in 1958. A few rounds of these well-received addresses over two years and a professorial vacancy resulted in a faculty appointment at his beloved alma mater in 1751, and following his required subscription to the Westminster Confession before the presbytery of Glasgow, Smith was installed as the University of Glasgow's professor of logic and rhetoric at the age of twenty-seven. He moved on, in 1752, to the newly vacated and illustrious chair of moral philosophy previously held (until 1745) by his former teacher, the "never to be forgotten Hutcheson." During this most productive period of his life, Smith also served in college administration, but did not neglect involvement in multiple learned societies and social connections in both Glasgow and Edinburgh. The latter was also the center of Scottish economic, political, and cultural affairs, and his frequent visits there and the elite crowd with whom he fraternized resulted in several things, chief of which was his lifelong friendship with David Hume and his exposure to the reigning economic paradigm of the day, mercantilism. For all his rather plain looks, curious personal habits, and hypochondria evidenced at length in his correspondence, particularly to his mother, Smith knew to rub shoulders with the upper crust. He could certainly be gracious in social and business circles, and his published work often preceded him. He had the cosmopolitan outlook so characteristic of other key figures in Scotland's intellectual, cultural, political, and economic milieu, and he absorbed the political, economic, and social forms he found. As Jerry Muller puts it, in such a stimulating environment, "it is no wonder that Scottish intellectuals in Edinburgh and Glasgow were given to reflecting on the 'stages' of society and the role of government and commerce in the movement from one stage to another."[13] This is an apt description of the structure and underlying motive of *WN*.

Eight years following his Glasgow appointment, Smith's lectures on moral philosophy culminated in book form in London in 1759. It was a topic with which he was concerned his entire life. *TMS* went through six editions, the most substantive changes being made for the second (1761) and the final (1790) versions. The former included responses to criticism from David Hume, while the latter, released shortly before his death, was a major overhaul. Interpreting this long, thirty-one-year history of revision in Smith's moral philosophy has added complexity to Smithian studies and rendered them less conclusive. One heavily redacted area in the sixth edition concerns the role of religion and Smith's apparently changed views in this area. Through successive editions, the concept of the "impartial spectator" received improved nuancing as well. Publication of *TMS* established Adam Smith's international reputation as a leading moral philosopher, and the fame that came with it connected Smith well with the literary and social circles in Edinburgh and everywhere in Europe.

13. Muller, *Adam Smith*, 23.

The book can be explained as an essay directed to the literate cohort of society: intellectuals, thinkers, and the educated public generally. In his summary of the "making" of *TMS,* Ross attends to interesting details regarding the anticipation of *TMS* by some anxious individuals and the positive reception by those to whom the initial copies were sent. There was some criticism as well, which had been invited by Adam Smith himself: "I am now about publishing a new edition of my Book, and would be greatly obliged to you for any criticisms."[14] Such an invitation demonstrated the epistemic humility that intellects of Smith's stature often lack.

The essay engages in the intellectual and emotional dissection of "virtue" and examines its relation to moral behavior, using explanations derived from social science. Smith's project in *TMS* has been labeled a "science of morals"; it employs his doctrine of "sympathy" as the organizing principle in the formation of moral sentiments. The closely related concept that Smith introduces at the very beginning of his ethical theory is the value and place of the "impartial spectator."[15] This "spectator theory of moral judgement" communicates the importance of impartiality and underscores the disinterested character of the moral standpoint. This not entirely new conception of the "impartial spectator" would later mature into Smith's philosophy of conscience.[16]

This system of thought in moral theory has precedent in the views of his teacher Hutcheson and his close friend Hume, although Smith builds considerably on these earlier foundations. He also drew upon the contributions of the bishop of Durham, Joseph Butler (1692–1752), who spoke to the authoritative nature of conscience. It has been pointed out that the vast improvement of Adam Smith's conceptions over his predecessors' is that Smith's idea is cast within a broader framework that explains the source and nature of

14. Ross, *Life,* 157–94; *Corr.,* 49.

15. *TMS,* 26 ff.

16. *TMS,* 130–31, 134–37.

conscience. To such a system of moral theory, "impartiality" is a necessary and sufficient condition, since the spectator is not personally involved in the adjudicative process. This enables disinterested reflection upon a person's own behavior. *TMS* manifests Smith's skill in systematizing moral philosophy through codifying existing work and making creative contributions regarding the moral sense in the construction of a systematic whole.

Smith also lectured on jurisprudence, which included law, government, and political economy, thus planting the seeds for his much later work, *WN*, which drew primarily from the material he delivered on political economy. The already mentioned student notes on law and government were found later, one set as late as 1958, and these became *LJ*.

## Tutor to the Upper Crust

To the university's great regret, Smith resigned his post in 1764, thus marking the end of his life in the academy. His tenure and prominence at the University of Glasgow and the popularity of his *TMS* had brought Smith into contact, not only with fellow scholars, but also with many business and government leaders. Smith was made the irresistible offer of a financially secure future as tutor and chaperone to Europe-bound, eighteen-year-old Henry Scott, the Duke of Buccleuch, by his prominent stepfather, Charles Townshend, MP, Chancellor of the Exchequer.[17] This brought Smith to the European continent, where he moved in the exclusive world of intellectuals, merchants, and the political elite, many of international renown. He visited and resided in multiple places: Toulouse, Geneva (where he met Voltaire), and Paris, where, within the circles of the French Enlightenment intelligentsia, he was introduced to economists Anne-Robert-Jacques Turgot

17. Ross, *Life*, 151; *Corr.*, 95.

(1727–81) and François Quesnay (1694–1774). While the former was a prominent politician, the latter was the royal physician to Louis XV and the primary intellectual inspiration behind the physiocratic school of economics.

## On a Fading Economic Order

The hustle and bustle of Edinburgh were closely related, in economic affairs, to the rapid rate of growth of eighteenth-century Great Britain and Europe in the struggle to emerge from widespread poverty into a new age.[18] Adam Smith would have associated much with the merchant class, after whom he pejoratively christened the current hegemonic economic arrangement called the "mercantile system" that dominated the entire early modern period. At the same time, a recent system of economic affairs—physiocracy—was also contending for respectability, but it lasted only briefly. Mercantilism was much more dangerous and damaging.

Adam Smith opposed the principles, philosophies, and policies that promoted these two erring systems of economic management and censured them severely, a critique that constitutes a quarter of *WN*. Both systems, for entirely different reasons, resulted in truncated economic production, resulting in restricted expansion and wealth creation. The first order of the business of political economy, began Smith, in reviewing and then building "Systems of political Œconomy," is to provide subsistence for the people—or, more

18. This section draws primarily from Stanley L. Brue and Randy R. Grant, eds., *The Evolution of Economic Thought*, 8th ed. (Mason, OH: South-Western, 2013); Heinz D. Kurz, *Economic Thought: A Brief History*, trans. Jeremiah Riemer (New York: Columbia University Press, 2016); Muller, *Adam Smith*; Ross, *Life*; Hanley, *Adam Smith: His Life*; Knud Haakonssen, ed., *The Cambridge Companion to Adam Smith* (Cambridge: Cambridge University Press, 2006); Laura LaHaye, "Mercantilism," https://www.econlib.org/library/Enc/Mercantilism.html.

precisely, to facilitate people's self-sufficiency in the provision of such subsistence. Its second object is to ensure a sufficient revenue flow to the commonwealth for the provision of public services. Political economy, therefore, "proposes both to enrich the people and the sovereign."[19]

## Back to Kirkcaldy, Then Briefly London

Tutoring the young duke and being his traveling companion on the continent for two years was good for both parties. While the student learned from the master, Smith's social skills were developed, along with an ever-expanding network of key political and social connections. Returning to Kirkcaldy—his "retreat," Hume called it—he made substantial progress on *WN*, all the while releasing new editions of *TMS*. Activating the handsome pension facilitated by Townshend a few years earlier, he moved on to London in 1773 to put the final touches on *WN* and had such severe fits of ill health (fatigue) and hypochondria that he made David Hume his literary executor soon after he got there, fearing he lay at death's door.[20]

*WN* came off the press on March 9, 1776, to high acclaim. Upon his receipt of the book, Hugh Blair (1718–1800), an Edinburgh cleric in the "moderate" camp, offered it high praise: *WN* "will in some degree become, the Commercial Code of Nations," he declared, even if it required certain amendments and corrections.[21] Likewise, David Hume was highly congratulatory ("Euge! Belle!"), which does not mean he thought it perfect.[22]

19. *WN*, 428–662.

20. *Corr.*, 168. Smith left all his "literary papers" with Hume; none were "worth the publishing," but some "fragments" on the history of astronomy (*HA*) were published posthumously and appeared in *EPS*, 31–105.

21. *Corr.*, 187–90.

22. *Corr.*, 186–87, written April 1, 1776, a few months before his death on August 25.

The dissemination and widespread reading of the masterpiece, in conjunction with other felicitous events, opened yet more avenues. Smith was appointed a Commissioner of Customs for Scotland in 1777. This career step adds a touch of both irony and curiosity to this already intriguing narrative. It was ironic to have a passionate advocate of free trade, who passed much of his life and energy offering a radical critique of the existing economic order, close his career in the government division responsible for collecting revenues from the control of trade. And, curiously, the father he never knew, also named Adam Smith, similarly ended his days as an official in the Customs service.

Adam Smith was welcomed to London, where government officials sought his advice on economic policy, particularly regarding international trade. Throughout these discussions, he maintained the fundamental principle of political economy by which all nations and individuals flourish: free trade. His advice resulted in changed government policy. He spoke at length about the economic fray of British mercantilist policies in the American colonies. He sided with the colonial position and was in accord with Benjamin Franklin, whom, according to circumstantial evidence, he had met often and to whom he had read portions of *WN* that came out in a second edition in 1778.[23]

## Edinburgh and the End

Retrieving his mother from Kirkcaldy, Smith relocated to a historic district in Edinburgh named Canongate, a cultural center of the Scottish Enlightenment. Here Smith spent the last twelve years of his life, publishing editions three to five of *WN*: 1784, 1786, and 1789. The third (1784) edition is the most substantial revision of all, with significant reworking of existing material and

23. Ross, *Life*, 255–56.

the addition of substantial new work, particularly to the section on international trade. The differences between all other editions and their immediate predecessors are slight.

Smith's mother died in 1784, followed a few years later in 1788 by the passing of his cousin Janet Douglas, a longtime companion of his mother. In early 1790, his final and crowning work on moral philosophy resulted in the release of a revised and expanded edition of *TMS*. Adam Smith died on July 17, 1790, expressing a sentiment not uncommon among many great scholars: that his lifetime scholarly contributions were rather paltry. He was interred in Canongate Kirkyard. His wish, that all of his unpublished and surviving work be destroyed by fire, was honored a few days later.

## Smith's Social Imaginary and Religion

Scottish Enlightenment scholar Gordon Graham concludes that we cannot, with absolute certainty, adjudicate on the question of Smith's personal faith.[24] But what is unambiguously clear is that it did not look anything like traditional Christian spirituality. On a second question—whether Smith engaged any theological categories—Graham finds that his providentialism demonstrated a sort of "thin 'deism,'" not unlike that of David Hume. Despite Smith's use of commonly understood theological concepts like "omniscience" and "omnipotence"—concepts associated with what is called "theology proper" in any traditional theological curriculum—his use is not an explicitly Christian one. Graham's assessment is that Smith's self-understanding was certainly not

24. Gordon Graham, "Adam Smith and Religion," in Hanley, *Adam Smith: His Life*, 305–20. See also a closely related essay by Ryan Patrick Hanley, "Bringing Religion Back In: Remarks on Gordon Graham," *Journal of Scottish Philosophy* 17, no. 1 (2019): 6–12, at https://www.researchgate.net/publication/331578130_Bringing_Religion_Back_In_Remarks_on_Gordon_Graham_for_the_Journal_of_Scottish_Philosophy.

that of a theologian, and neither should we evaluate him as such. He concludes that Smith's focus is really on philosophical anthropology: First, true religion is sourced in human nature and plays a role in the progression of social life. Second, the benefits of true religion are centered in people's psychological and moral lives; their moral sentiments are implanted as deeply as the appetite for more basic human needs like food and sex. Smith also asserts that because moral rules are really laws of a deity, they work to the general good.[25] Graham's focus on Adam Smith and other luminaries of the day has helped us reappreciate the value of religion in Enlightenment Scotland.

Intensive research into the complicated and irregular landscape of Adam Smith's metaphysic, including his social, intellectual, religious, and economic world as it existed, not only in eighteenth-century Scotland, but throughout the places he visited on the European continent, demonstrates that Smith was a man through whom many religious and philosophical threads were woven together into a rich and colorful tapestry.[26] He was raised a Calvinist, was exposed to the morphed Presbyterianism of the Moderate party at university in Glasgow, and appropriated much of the Stoicism of Marcus Aurelius in his intellectual and philosophical journey. His resulting religious convictions can best be described as a rich mixture of deism and natural theology, interspersed with some sparsely released sprinklings of Reformed (Calvinist) orthodoxy. About Adam Smith's personal religious commitment and its transformation over the course of a fruitful life, we are, in the end, left guessing. But the next two chapters will show that much of his thought aligned with the social imaginary and *practical* faith of the Reformed Christian.

25. *TMS*, 161–63, referenced in Graham, "Smith and Religion," 313.

26. See my forthcoming "Adam Smith (1723–90): Social Imaginary and Religion," in *Pro Rege*, March 2025.

# 3

# HUMAN NATURE AND MORAL PHILOSOPHY

Adam Smith's moral philosophy is detailed in his already mentioned *Theory of Moral Sentiments* (1759–1790), wherein he outlines the principles of human nature that characterize the ideal society. The claim appearing in the opening paragraph, that concern for the well-being of one's neighbor is a constitutive element in optimizing one's own happiness, alerts us to the nature of this work. But so does the rarely mentioned subtitle introduced in the fourth edition of 1774 and maintained through the sixth and last edition of 1790: *An Essay towards an Analysis of the Principles by which Men naturally judge concerning the Conduct and Character, first of their Neighbours, and afterwards of themselves.*[1]

This establishes *TMS* as an architectonically social project. That this would be Smith's personal orientation is to be expected since his early Glaswegian education instilled in him the view

1. D. D. Raphael and A. L. Macfie, "Introduction," in *TMS*, 40.

that humanity is innately social, a position commonly held since Aristotle. From Hutcheson and others, he learned that morality was cultivated in the social arena—a conviction that self-consciously countered the view held in the emerging discipline of natural law that human action is propelled by selfishness. This had been promoted by Thomas Hobbes, an early progenitor of that tradition.[2] As we shall see in chapter 4, Adam Smith was not entirely free of this principle. Nonetheless, his use of it in his writing on political economy is highly nuanced.

In common with the evolution of intellectual history generally, there was, of course, a developing tradition that helped shape Smith's contributions to ethical and moral theory. However, while Smith interacted with Enlightenment thinkers of the day, such as Lord Kames, Bishop Butler, Bernard Mandeville, and Jean-Jacques Rousseau, and while their thought receives significant consideration in his work, the ideas of his teacher Francis Hutcheson and his close friend David Hume contribute the foundational elements of Smith's moral philosophy, much of which is found here by extension, correction, and opposition. For example, in answer to the overarching question, "How do people make moral judgements?" Smith maintained, with both Hutcheson and Hume, that moral action is not an exercise of rational faculties, but rather an expression of natural feelings: "Moral action is motivated by the disinterested feeling of benevolence, and moral judgement expresses the disinterested feeling of approval or disapproval."[3] Humanity, taught Hutcheson, was able to exercise moral judgment in social intercourse by something he called somewhat vaguely the "moral sense." By this he meant some inexplicable, special sense that a neutral observer exercises in determining the morality of particular actions and

2. Among others, Ian Simpson Ross makes this link in *The Life of Adam Smith* (Oxford: Oxford University Press, 1995), 161.

3. Raphael and Macfie, "Introduction," 10–12.

behaviors. And this observer would judge that sentiment good only if it were also benevolent.[4]

Hume improved on this explanation of moral adjudication by noting that something as complicated as moral motivation cannot be completely explained by the disinterested approval of the neutral observer. He introduced the much more specific concept of "sympathy" as that quality or sentiment in human nature capable of such judgment. For Hume, sympathy was very specifically assigned to the feelings of pleasure and pain that an agent—the person affected by an action to which he is reacting—was experiencing. It was this reaction that was observed by the neutral party.[5]

Recognizing even greater complexity than Hume, the Smithian turn in this developing tradition of moral philosophy centered on the much broader meaning he assigned to the feeling of sympathy. For Smith, the sympathetic capacity involves the sharing of any feeling, not just pleasure and pain. Further, sympathy's first job in moral approval is to examine the agent's motive (as it was also with Hutcheson and Hume). What has priority in moral judgments—intention or the act arising from the intention? Smith believed that pure motives issue in approval of an agent's action as proper.[6] Ultimately the attitude behind a particular behavior is what receives the spectator's approval or censure, rather than the results of the act itself. As Smith puts it in another context, "What chiefly enrages us against the man who injures or insults us is the little account which he seems to make of us, the unreasonable preference which he gives to himself above us, and that absurd self-love, by which he seems to imagine, that other people may be sacrificed at any time, to his conveniency or his humour."[7]

4. Raphael and Macfie, "Introduction," 10–12.
5. Raphael and Macfie, "Introduction," 10–12.
6. Raphael and Macfie, "Introduction," 11–15.
7. *TMS*, 96.

In this connection, the term "sentiment" in the book's title and throughout the text requires some explanation. Nowhere does Smith explain what he means by this term, but throughout his work it is used interchangeably with feelings, emotions, passions, and more.[8] Interestingly, Smith does devote a few pages near the end of his work to inquire what aspect of human nature or "power or faculty of mind" or "contrivance or mechanism within" enables us to judge the behavior or conduct of our fellow humanity. What facilitates our approval or disapproval of another's actions? He traces three different accounts of this. Some maintain that we approve or disapprove of our own or others' conduct out of self-love; others hold that it is reason—the faculty by which we distinguish truth from falsehood; while a third group argues that it is our "immediate sentiment and feeling." Smith devotes over double the space to this third explanation and, as a committed empiricist and with much refinement, he identifies with its proponents, of which Hutcheson and Hume are key representatives.[9]

The inherently social nature of humanity means, for Smith and the tradition he furthers, that questions of morality and acceptable behavior are determined and adjudicated, not in isolation, but in relationship. Codes of behavior arise empirically from within humanity itself through the give-and-take of regular interaction. The empirical foundation of such socialization means that something other than a written moral code or an established rule of law constitutes that against which all behavior should be checked. In other words, while the socialization of the individual in Smith's moral theory is accomplished outside of foundational rules and eternally abiding principles, even one's rational faculties cannot

8. As pointed out by Eric Schliesser, "The Theory of Moral Sentiments," in *Adam Smith: His Life, Thought, and Legacy*, ed. Ryan Patrick Hanley (Princeton, NJ: Princeton University Press, 2016), 34–36.

9. *TMS*, 314–27. However, he offhandedly acknowledges that this exercise is of no practical consequence, but "is a mere matter of philosophical curiosity" (*TMS*, 315).

be relied upon to judge accurately the rightness or wrongness of behavior. Smith was a committed empiricist; he left little space for rationalist philosophy.

Our analysis of Smith's moral philosophy and its value for the twenty-first century individual operating in the Christian, post-Reformational tradition, will commence with examining his famous opening statement and will proceed from there by exploring the epistemological categories and anthropological assumptions that drive his moral theory and virtue ethics. This thematic summary of *TMS* commences with Smith's unique view of self-interest, unpacks the similarly distinctive Smithean conception of sympathy, examines the pivotal role of the "impartial spectator," and addresses the necessity and action of the imagination. This leads to a brief introduction of Smith's virtue ethics and explains the failure of the "social mirror" in a phenomenologically constructed system of morality. Then, in the final section, the adjudicating function of something called "conscience" is examined. The chapter closes with a critical analysis and assessment of the value of Smith's moral philosophy for the contemporary Reformed Christian believer.

## Thematic Analysis of Smith's Moral Philosophy

*TMS* is an elaboration of Smith's opening thesis, which sketches humanity's relational and dynamic interplay in the architecture of a system of ethics that, ultimately, constitutes a virtuous society. It is thus a project studying people's communal interplay, the "social processes by which the egoistic passions are channeled, moderated, and redirected, making it possible for men to live peaceably with others, pursue their happiness with foresight, and act altruistically."[10] Smith explains:

10. Jerry Z. Muller, *Adam Smith in His Time and Ours* (Princeton, NJ: Princeton University Press, 1995), 99.

> How selfish soever man may be supposed, there are evidently some principles in his nature, which interest him in the fortune of others, and render their happiness necessary to him, though he derives nothing from it except the pleasure of seeing it. Of this kind is pity or compassion, the emotion which we feel for the misery of others, when we either see it, or are made to conceive it in a very lively manner. That we often derive sorrow from the sorrow of others, is a matter of fact too obvious to require any instances to prove it.[11]

## Self-Interest

Despite our innate concern for others' welfare, humans by virtue of their createdness naturally tend most to their own happiness. With the Stoics, Smith declares that "by nature . . . every man . . . is first and principally recommended to his own care."[12] Because interpersonal relations center on a shared sympathy, our concern for others' happiness naturally causes us to be concerned for our own—truly shared sympathy presupposes concern for our own happiness. But the relational character of humanity means that, for Smith, one's happiness includes others' well-being. Consequently, we consider not only our own emotions in our behavior and sentiments, but also the emotions of others. This includes a disinterested adjudication of our own behavior. We are checks on our own behaviors through the constant exercise of self-command, lest we offend the disinterested observer or fall short of the expectations of that spectator. Attending "the great school of self-command" is a lifelong endeavor, since the acquisition of moral agency is gradual and begins from childhood at home.[13]

11. *TMS*, 9.
12. *TMS*, 219.
13. *TMS*, 145–47; on pp. 145–56, Smith argues that the exercise of self-command is a duty, while the emphasis on pp. 237–64 is upon the practice of self-command as a virtue.

If we faithfully exercise our duty of self-command, it takes on a form of virtue. Constant accommodation to others' emotions through the ongoing practice of self-control makes us better at tempering our activity to receive the approbation we so desperately seek. A disinterested force guarantees that people moderate their sentiments to approximate what others' sentiments might be. Because we are social creatures, there is a certain mutuality in our social interaction.

But Smith does admit that there is a prioritizing within this reciprocity. The "perfection of human nature" is demonstrated by the dominance of our "benevolent affections" over our "selfish" ones. In other words, we must consider others' welfare over our own. Benevolence trumps selfishness, whether by the propositional truth of, say, Christianity, or the phenomenological process of human society. Both deliver the same end result. The Christian faith urges us "to love our neighbour as we love ourselves," says Smith, but how is that different from a naturally constructed moral psychology which holds that it is through social experiences that "we love ourselves only as we love our neighbour?" The moral behavior taught by "the great precept of nature" is identical to that prescribed by "the great law of Christianity."[14] The one authority is on a par with the other.[15] We become moral through obedience to foundational rules; we become equally moral through the natural process of social experiences, because trying to share the feelings of others as closely as possible is one of our main drives. And being true to both "systems" of morality requires a healthy dose of self-command to counteract our natural egoism.[16] If, as we

14. *TMS*, 25.

15. As noted by Raphael and Macfie in "Introduction," *TMS*, 23n1. The editors of *TMS* observe that Smith combines the Christian ethic of law with the Stoic ethic of self-command.

16. It is for this reason that Muller, in *Adam Smith*, 103, posits that *TMS* is more a book about self-control than it is about sympathy.

shall see in *WN*, the drive to engage in the interchange of market activity is for reasons of self-improvement from the perspective of material well-being, in an analogous fashion the motivation of human emotional interchange is the pleasure received from mutual sympathy. For "nothing pleases us more than to observe in other men a fellow-feeling with all the emotions of our own breast; nor are we ever so much shocked as by the appearance of the contrary."[17]

## Sympathy

The notion of sympathy conceptualized by Smith speaks much to his understanding of human nature and is determinative in the establishing of his normative moral theory. Sympathy is a key element in determining acceptable behavior in interpersonal relationships. Smith observes that the sympathetic process exists because people are intrigued by the very possibility of mutual sympathy. Mutual sympathy pleases us because it saddens us not to be able to sympathize with happiness or sorrow. Out of our concern for others, he avers, arises our desire to share the sorrow of one who is suffering—"it hurts us to find that we cannot share his uneasiness." The human compulsion for mutual sympathy is so strong that we are pleased when able to sympathize and hurt when unable.[18]

That is why the sympathetic process is central to the construction of Smith's system of morality. But we must understand "sympathy" in a particular fashion, which is more akin to the way we understand "empathy" today. Traditionally, notes Smith, "sympathy" related to our "fellow feeling" with others' sorrow, a sense of pity or compassion for their situation. Smith defines it more broadly: as a state of mind by which we "denote our fellow

17. *TMS*, 13.
18. *TMS*, 15–16.

feeling *with any passion* whatever."[19] Scholars generally affirm the multipurpose use to which the word is applied by Smith: pity for others, a natural "fellow-feeling" one has with others, emotional or sentimental similitude, the well-known maxim: walking a mile in another person's shoes, etc. Every moral judgment in social interaction, and the subsequent code of behavior arising from these adjudications, is the result of this sympathetic process, which explains the various captions used to explain Smith's moral theory or moral psychology as one of "reflective sentimentalism," "sophisticated emotivism," "cognitive feeling," and the like.[20] Although all these labels reflect some truth, for Smith moral phenomenology is normative moral theory.

To emphasize, the predominance of this concept in Smith's system arises from his conviction that an inherent quality in human nature is the desire to see one's neighbor do well. Significantly, however, this is a wholly unselfish desire; our selfless interest in another's well-being is motivated by nothing other than his or her flourishing, regardless of how this may advantage me personally.

It has been pointed out that Smith's use of the concept of "selfish" or "selfishness" is actually quite broad—double-barreled, as it were. We fail to understand the true inner workings of Smith's moral psychology if we see the condition of selfishness in the traditional way—as only an ethical or moral issue. To this we must add an epistemic dimension: that being able to see the situation of another means that we are able to transcend our own personal emotional and psychological situatedness and jump the epistemic gap required to enter, inhabit, and understand the world

19. *TMS*, 10; emphasis added.

20. Noted by Christel Fricke, "Adam Smith: The Sympathetic Process and the Origin and Function of Conscience," in *The Oxford Handbook of Adam Smith*, ed. Christopher J. Berry, Maria Pia Paganelli, and Craig Smith (Oxford: University Press, 2013), 174. See also Alexander Broadie, "Sympathy and the Impartial Spectator, " in *The Cambridge Companion to Adam Smith*, ed. Knud Haakonssen (Cambridge: Cambridge University Press, 2006), 158–88.

of another. The resulting emotional equilibrium between the agent and the spectator—this blending of the ethical and epistemic horizons—yields the requisite social harmony for successful execution of Smith's program of ethical inquiry, based as it is on his analysis of human sociability.[21]

We must understand the notion of "sympathy" in a similar fashion. On its narrow interpretation, sympathy taps into the emotional dimension of the human psyche and is limited to the idea of sharing another's feelings. In a broader sense, though, sympathy represents the conduit through which emotions are conveyed and understood. "Pity and compassion," explains Smith, "are words appropriated to signify our fellow feeling with the sorrow of others. Sympathy, though its meaning was, perhaps, originally the same, may now . . . be made use of to denote our fellow-feeling with any passion whatever."[22] Smith uses these two meanings almost interchangeably in the same fashion as he employs the dual meaning of selfishness.[23] Finally, it is this further extension that facilitates an individual's self-awareness of the sharing of another person's feelings.[24]

This situates the two parties—the agent and the spectator—on an emotionally level playing field, as it were. Even if the individual being observed is "altogether incapable" of expressing a passionate response to a particular set of circumstances or state of affairs, the sympathetic drive within the spectator causes a passion to arise in the breast, actuated by the imagination, that enables such response.[25] The spectator has deeper insight into the

21. I am indebted for these insights to Charles L. Griswold Jr., *Adam Smith and the Virtues of Enlightenment* (Cambridge: Cambridge University Press, 1999), 78.

22. *TMS*, 10.

23. Griswold notes that "Smith occasionally slides back and forth between the narrow and broad meanings of the term, and so between what might in a Christian tradition be thought of as a laudable sentiment or virtue and a notion in moral psychology with bearing on epistemic issues" (*Virtues of Enlightenment*, 79).

24. Ross, *Life*, 164.

25. *TMS*, 12.

emotional status of the agent experiencing an event than does the agent himself.

This powerful human drive for emotional harmony—"mutual sympathy," Smith calls it—comes about as a given from the way Smith understands human nature. Our sympathy for others clearly enlivens our joy; conversely, it also attenuates our grief. "This correspondence of the sentiments of others with our own appears to be a cause of pleasure, and the want of it a cause of pain."[26] Moreover, it is not only actual circumstances and the associated emotional states that evoke such sympathy. It is, in fact, any passion to which the mind of man can lend itself. Sympathy can be aroused by simply "the view of a certain emotion in another person," from expressions of grief and joy to a smiling face indicating the agent's response to good or bad fortune. But feelings of anger are not so easily entered into. By nature, the spectator is oriented to oppose such sentiment until at least informed of the cause.[27] Even "fellow-feeling" has its limits.

Scholars have noted Smith's desire to have his moral philosophy understood through his abundant use of examples from real life, history, and even graphic descriptions that conjure up in any reader certain passions and evoke sympathetic sentiments in the reader—feelings of happiness or sorrow, relish or disgust, etc. Smith's assertion that the spectator may, at times, observe an agent's true state even though that person may be unable to recognize it himself is illustrated with this visceral example:

> Of all the calamities to which the condition of mortality exposes mankind, the loss of reason appears, to those who have the least spark of humanity, by far the most dreadful, and they behold that last stage of human wretchedness with deeper

26. *TMS*, 14.
27. *TMS*, 11.

> commiseration than any other. But the poor wretch, who is in it, laughs and sings perhaps, and is altogether insensible of his own misery. The anguish which humanity feels, therefore, at the sight of such an object, cannot be the reflection of any sentiment of the sufferer. The compassion of the spectator must arise altogether from the consideration of what he himself would feel if he was reduced to the same unhappy situation, and, what perhaps is impossible, was at the same time able to regard it with his present reason and judgment.[28]

The contemporary relevance of this remarkable eighteenth-century insight into the inner workings of the human psyche is clearly seen in cases of brain diseases, such as the progressive neurodegenerative condition we call Alzheimer's disease.

Through the workings of the sympathetic process, humankind's sense of propriety is determined. It is this feeling of sympathy that drives moral sentiments and is foundational to proper and thus commendable behavior. This natural regard for others' sentiments acts as guardrails to our own behavior. The best way to approximate someone else's feeling or motive is to imagine ourselves in a similar situation.[29] This conception of others' feelings and motives means that the imagination is central in coming to such an empathetic determination of, say, another person's sensations of pain or pleasure. "Changing places in fancy with the sufferer"[30] (even if the sufferer is unaware of his own situation or condition, as the example above illustrates) is the only means of generating empathy, which should be the goal of every "attentive spectator." And because the key to legitimate feelings of sympathy is impartiality, the spectator is to be not only "attentive" but also "impartial." Sympathy cannot be detached from being an impartial spectator.

28. *TMS*, 12.
29. *TMS*, 9.
30. *TMS*, 10.

## The Impartial Spectator

As with other Smithian concepts and ideas, the vast literature associated with the mysterious notion of the disinterested adjudicating force called "the impartial spectator" has done little to demystify the enigma. Smith introduces what he initially calls the "disinterested observer" somewhat casually early on in *TMS* as someone who would strike a note of familiarity with all of us. This takes on a more formal nature as his moral theory itself is unfolded.[31]

The concept of the impartial spectator "helps to bring out the disinterested character of the moral standpoint."[32] Distance from the agent ensures a certain degree of detachment required for neutrality in judgment. Although the spectator is not personally involved in the situation of the agent, that does not mean that the interaction between the agent and the spectator is meaningless.[33] It means rather that humanity—social to the core—is endowed with a natural moral drive that responds to behavioral stimuli. In Smith's moral philosophy, those stimuli are responsive to others' assessment of one's emotional state; conversely, others' emotional condition is affected by our adjudication. The spectator's approval (or disapproval) of the agent's response to a situation brings the agent pleasure (or displeasure). For example, an agent's demonstrated concern for others—say, helping the poor—brings approbation from the impartial spectator, while ignoring the poor is seen to do harm and results in censure. People learn to align their emotional state of being with the expectations of the impartial spectator. This means that individuals moderate—rein in, if need be—their behavior to comport with the expectations of others. At this point, says Smith, any typical disinterested person—that impartial spectator—would empathize with us. Any positive behavior that demonstrates concern for others would meet with

31. Compare *TMS* Parts I and II with Part III.
32. Raphael and Macfie, "Introduction," 15.
33. Raphael and Macfie, "Introduction," 14.

the approval of the impartial spectator. And from that approval we derive pleasure. "Nothing pleases us more than to observe in other men a fellow-feeling with all the emotions of our own breast; nor are we ever so much shocked as by the appearance of the contrary."[34]

Impartiality is the *sine qua non* in the arbitration of moral disagreement that arises because humanity is biased by nature. Even though we are instructed to consider others before considering ourselves, we naturally love ourselves above others and seek our own welfare first. Our self-love is what drives us. Given that "every man . . . is much more deeply interested in whatever immediately concerns himself, than in what concerns any other man,"[35] no one is truly unbiased in decisions concerning moral right and wrong, and it is impossible for situations to be observed neutrally. We do the best we can by imagining ourselves in the other's situation because by nature we have the capacity to imagine others' sentiments—how they think and feel.

Here again Smith nuances elements of a developing moral philosophy beyond that of his predecessors—primarily Hutcheson and Hume. His description of the impartial spectator demonstrates the interdependency of the feelings that ought both to motivate our moral behavior and to judge others' sentiments. The sharing of others' feelings occurs, not just when we see them laugh or cry, but also when we imagine being in their place. Smith identifies this imaginative projection as "sympathy" and grants the imagination tremendous privilege in the development of moral capacities.[36]

These moral capacities are thus the judgments of the people, the society, surrounding us. The action of the impartial spectator helps us see ourselves objectively and is formative in our attainment

34. *TMS*, 13.

35. *TMS*, 82–83.

36. Noted by Samuel Fleischacker, *On Adam Smith's* Wealth of Nations*: A Philosophical Companion* (Princeton, NJ: Princeton University Press, 2005), 46.

of moral and aesthetic maturity.[37] In turn, our moral and aesthetic maturity is marked by internalizing the values and expectations of our community, since the impartial spectator judges by the norms of that society in which one has been socialized. Such mutual sympathy is foundational to an orderly society. This represents an underlying presupposition of Smith's political philosophy: "Man it has been said, has a natural love for society, and desires that the union of mankind should be preserved for its own sake, and though he himself was to derive no benefit from it. The orderly and flourishing state of society is agreeable to him, and he takes delight in contemplating it."[38] That moral development results from such social interaction is a natural outcome of Smith's view of humanity. Humanity is happiest in society when moral standards are met. And it is society's influence that transforms people into moral beings.

## Imagination

The sympathetic imagination was a common feature of the literature of sensibility in Smith's day.[39] He maintained that our senses have limitations. They can never take us beyond or outside ourselves. Our loved one may be in pain, but "as long as we ourselves are at our ease, our senses will never inform us of what he suffers."[40] The imagination does all the work, copying the impressions of our own senses. This imaginative projection is very much what Smith means by "sympathy" and distinguishes the further nuancing in his developing understanding of moral capacity from that of Hume and Hutcheson.[41]

The distinction between imagination and reality is genuine. The imaginative machinations involved in closing the previously

37. *TMS*, 110–12.
38. *TMS*, 88.
39. Ross, *Life*, 164.
40. *TMS*, 9.
41. Asserted by Fleischacker, *Philosophical Companion*, 46.

mentioned epistemic gap are a necessary condition to ensure some degree of accuracy in the measurement of the agent's emotional state brought on by the situation at hand. Only when the sympathetic spectator can accurately reconstruct the situation that brought about the agent's emotional state, can true empathy take place. "As we have no immediate experience of what other men feel, we can form no idea of the manner in which they are affected, but by conceiving what we ourselves should feel in the like situation."[42] Smith is concerned that our feelings on others' behalf may not match their feelings. We do the best we can, but Smith rightly maintains the distinction between imagination and reality. A mismatch of sentiment will debilitate social bonding and could replace that with social fracture. This would leave one of our main drives in life unfulfilled. This explains Smith's further claim that the agent—the "person principally concerned"—must help the spectator in this task of sympathizing by moderating the sharpness of his passion's "natural tone" to a pitch accessible to the spectator.[43] Toning down his emotional excess gives the agent practice in the central virtue of self-command. For his part, the spectator gains experience in practicing the virtue of benevolence by returning a deeper emotional response. And even then the spectator's imaginative powers yield, at best, only an approximation to the actual experience of the agent that brought about his feelings, whether good or ill. In short, the spectator will respond with empathetic fellow-feelings toward the agent based on the former's imagining being that agent—actually *becoming* the agent. To optimize fellow-feeling, spectators must become agents and appropriate agents' feelings as their own. Smith maintains that such capacity for commiseration with fellow humanity is possessed by all men and women to a greater or

42. *TMS*, 9.
43. *TMS*, 22.

lesser degree—the "virtuous and humane" as well as the "greatest ruffian, the most hardened violator of the laws of society."[44]

Access to another person's world is crucial if we are to be effective as impartial spectators.[45] This is where the agent's narrative is being written; this is the scene of his situatedness, giving rise to his perspective and his constellation of emotions. And this access is gained by the spectator's imagination. Our imaginative sympathy, although capable of picturing a sheer physical condition or a state of being, still falls far short of the agent's true feelings. The spectator must be "transported" into that state of being and bring it home to himself, thereby reliving the "drama" in his imagination. Smith explains this phenomenon something like this: We do not grow hungry simply by imagining the situation of a hungry person. We imagine ourselves truly starving. This may cause us dread when we, in this way, bring home to ourselves someone else's terrifying reality—true hunger. "The sympathetic imagination is not solely representational or reproductive. It is also narrative, always seeking . . . to draw things together into a coherent story, thus bringing the spectator out of himself and onto the larger stage. It is other seeking and poetic."[46]

## Virtue Ethics

This process of mutual emotional adjustment through the sympathetic act—reconfiguring our emotional dispositions or retuning them in response to observed misdirected motives and behaviors—gives rise to a model of virtue which Smith held to be much more than simply following moral rules.[47] In constructing his system of moral motivation and behavior, Smith constructed

44. *TMS*, 9.

45. Griswold, *Virtues of Enlightenment*, 116.

46. Griswold, *Virtues of Enlightenment*, 116.

47. Griswold notes that "the love of virtue is an outgrowth of sympathy" in *Virtues of Enlightenment*, 133.

a detailed model upon a simpler ethical framework developed earlier by David Hume and Joseph Butler.[48] Identifying virtue as a product of this ongoing exercise of emotional redesign, as described above, completes the social construction of the individual. Central to this system are general moral rules "ultimately founded upon experience of what, in particular instances, our moral faculties, our natural sense of merit and propriety, approve, or disapprove of."[49] That is the direction of causality in one's socialization: actions do not receive approval or disapproval because they conform to (or violate) some general rule. Rather, the general rule arises from the approval or disapproval of all behaviors in their particular circumstances.[50] The social construction of the individual is truly that—a theory of moral sentiments, a moral philosophy, an ethical code, built upon the phenomenological realities of living in human society.

Yet there is a place for Deity. It is through education, discipline, and example that regard for general rules of morality arise and conduct is affected. Such rules explain humans' sense of duty,

48. Samuel Fleischacker, "Adam Smith's Moral and Political Philosophy," *Stanford Encyclopedia of Philosophy* (November 11, 2020), https://plato.stanford.edu/entries/smith-moral-political/#SumSmiMor, 3.

49. *TMS*, 159.

50. For example, to the person who witnesses "an inhuman murder, committed from avarice, envy, or unjust resentment, and upon one too that loved and trusted the murderer, who beheld the last agonies of the dying person, who heard him, with his expiring breath, complain more of the perfidy and ingratitude of his false friend, than of the violence which had been done to him, there could be no occasion, in order to conceive how horrible such an action was, that he should reflect that one of the most sacred rules of conduct was what prohibited the taking away the life of an innocent person, that this was a plain violation of that rule and consequently a very blamable action. His detestation of this crime, it is evident, would arise instantaneously and antecedent to his having formed to himself any such general rule. The general rule, on the contrary, which he might afterwards form, would be founded upon the detestation which he felt necessarily arise in his own breast, at the thought of this, and every other particular action of the same kind" (*TMS*, 159–60). The heinousness of the action is determined by the circumstances surrounding it.

without which human society would "crumble into nothing." At first nature impresses, then reasoning and philosophy confirm, that moral rules are nothing other than the "commands and laws of the Deity, who will finally reward the obedient, and punish the transgressors of their duty."[51] Thus, general rules of morality may properly be called the laws of the Deity. This explains why the violence imparted to these general rules of morality through disobedience brings punishment upon the violator and excites indignation in the breast of every human spectator. A "new sacredness" attaches to general rules of morality when viewed as the laws of an "All-powerful Being," since now the merit and demerit of actions are determined by a code authored and enforced by Infinite Wisdom and Infinite Power. Humans are compelled by the strongest motives of self-interest to conform to the precepts of the moral code, lest they come under the punishment of God, the "great avenger of injustice."[52]

Bringing Deity into the equation stimulates conformity to common rules of conduct. In fact, such incentive to ethical behavior and enforcement of a "natural sense" of duty constitute a central benefit of religion. For while meritorious ethical behavior that aligns with socially constructed norms receives the imprimatur of the world, that same world places "a double confidence in the rectitude of the religious man's behavior."[53] It has been noted that Smith's emphasis upon a divinely oriented frame of reference for ethical behavior anticipates Kant's moral argument for belief in God without the conviction of his existence.[54] From chapter 2 we know that Smith held to some form of divinity.

We have seen that quite early in *TMS* Smith argues that the impartial spectator could most effectively sympathize with the

51. *TMS*, 163.
52. *TMS*, 161–70.
53. *TMS*, 170.
54. Fleischacker, "Smith's Moral and Political Philosophy," 4.

agent—"the person principally concerned"—if the "pitch" of that agent's passions were moderated to the degree that made them accessible to the spectator: "He must flatten . . . the sharpness of its natural tone, in order to reduce it to harmony and concord with the emotions" of the spectator. This was particularly necessary in cases of inconsolable pain and anger—situations that give rise to "violent and disagreeable passions." Indeed, such "concord" of sentiments is necessary and sufficient for "the harmony of society," Smith maintained.[55] Such behavior of the two parties evidences two different sets of virtues: the amiable (as in the case of the soft, gentle, and indulgent spectator) and the respectable (as evidenced by the self-denying and self-controlling agent). This illustration leads to Smith's conviction that "the propriety of every passion excited by objects peculiarly related to ourselves, the pitch which the spectator can go along with, must lie, it is evident, in a certain mediocrity."[56] The exercise of all passions inherent in human nature conduce most effectively to social well-being when moderated in their expression, since it is such moderation that enables the impartial spectator to sympathize with the agent. It is between the excesses and defects of all realms of human experience that propriety of conduct is found. Smith's system of virtue ethics bears strong resemblance to that of Aristotle; in fact, near the end of the volume, Smith notes that his system concerning the propriety and impropriety of conduct corresponds "pretty exactly" to that of the philosopher.[57]

While earlier accounts of Adam Smith's virtue ethics appear throughout *TMS*, it is not until Part VI of the sixth edition (1790) that we see the composite account and find ourselves reviewing the familiar territory of the cardinal virtues. Smith's entire system of moral behavior is centered on the rules of perfect prudence,

55. *TMS*, 21–23.
56. *TMS*, 27.
57. *TMS*, 271.

proper benevolence, and strict justice. But faithful practice of these virtues requires healthy doses of the "meta-virtue"[58] of self-command. Since our own passions and natural sensibilities derail us, we can see self-command as a psychological precondition to the exercise of any of them.[59] Haakonssen helpfully observes that while prudence concerns itself with the pursuit of our interests (and thus the subject of political economy), justice is geared toward the avoidance of injury to those interests (and thus the subject of jurisprudence).[60] Finally, while prudence, justice, and self-command build the ideal society and ensure its survival, it is the virtue of beneficence that promotes human flourishing in Smith's civilizing project.[61]

### The "Social Mirror" Malfunctions

As mentioned above, Smith's account of ethics and conscience is predicated on humanity's innate desire to please and, conversely, an inherent aversion to offend one's neighbor. All creatures are endowed with this psychological makeup. As a consequence, to be regarded favorably by one's neighbor bestows pleasure, while the opposite confers pain. Moreover, Nature endowed humanity with a desire for approval, but also a desire for being what ought to be approved of. While the first trait—the desire for approval—would prompt one to the affectation of virtue (and the concealment of vice), the second trait—being

58. This is Haakonssen's term; see his "Introduction: The Coherence of Smith's Thought," in Haakonssen, *Cambridge Companion*, 17.

59. Muller, *Adam Smith*, 97.

60. Haakonssen, "Introduction," 17–18.

61. The virtue of prudence received limited attention in the first five editions of *TMS*. Interestingly, editors Raphael and Macfie claim that "the more mature" Smith gave it significant coverage in the sixth edition because he had "pondered on economics so long" ("Introduction," 18). Recall the earlier observation that over his lifetime Smith spent considerably more time contemplating moral theory than political economy.

what ought to be approved of—is necessary in order to inspire one with the "real love of virtue, and with the real abhorrence of vice."[62] Desiring to be praiseworthy is as superior to praise as anxiety to be really fit for society is to appearances to be really fit. "But, though a wise man feels little pleasure from praise where he knows there is no praise-worthiness, he often feels the highest in doing what he knows to be praise-worthy, though he knows equally well that no praise is ever to be bestowed upon it."[63] To desire or accept praise where no praise is due can be the effect of only the most contemptible vanity. Authentic, praiseworthy character and behavior issue only from one who has a real love of virtue. All else is affectatious and inauthentic.

Smith presses home this distinction between praise and praiseworthiness for another reason. Men and women are naturally inclined to be virtuous, he maintains, because of their natural love of praiseworthiness. This requires that we view ourselves through the eyes of the impartial spectator, which alone can counter the attraction of self-love and vanity.[64] But Smith realizes that in adjudicating motive and behavior, the spectator is neither perfectly informed nor purely impartial. This results in poor discernment and mistaken judgments. Through experience we discover that sometimes we may have received (or given) undeserved praise; at other times we may have come under undeserved reproach. That is why praiseworthiness and blameworthiness, as barometers of behavior, motive, and character, are superior to simply receiving praise or blame. Because "the social 'mirror' often reflects badly,"[65] the role of conscience comes to claim a significant place in Smith's moral system, as has already been intimated.

62. *TMS*, 117.
63. *TMS*, 117.
64. Griswold, *Virtues of Enlightenment*, 130.
65. Griswold, *Virtues of Enlightenment*, 132.

## Conscience

The inevitable outcome of the dynamic interplay between agent and spectator is reflection upon their respective conduct. If someone is both hypothetical observer and agent, then he supposes himself to be the spectator of his own behavior and must imagine its effect upon himself. What are the sentiments and motives that give rise to his conduct? Answering this question involves establishing a certain degree of distance, and that is where the imagination plays a central role, since we must seek to view these sentiments through the eyes of other people if we are to give approbation or disapprobation to our own moral behavior. This involves, as it were, dividing oneself into two people. One becomes both agent and spectator, both the person judged and the judge. A solitary existence would yield no answer, since we need human society to provide the social mirror that facilitates such self-adjudication.[66] This exercise of seeking to determine what drives us is a learned behavior, since we soon come to realize that others adjudicate our motives and conduct, as we do theirs. Smith develops the idea of the impartial spectator to explain the source and nature of conscience,[67] which is the spectator's voice addressing the agent. Conscience, then, "the judge within," is a product of social relationship and is not a fact of reason, or even some innate moral sense as held by Hutcheson, but rather "an acquired form of moral self-awareness." In Smith's phenomenology of inner conflict, "moral struggle is our lot."[68] The self's relation to self is never impartial, but rather is always self-serving to the degree, asserts Smith, that "this self-deceit, this fatal weakness of mankind, is the source of half the disorders of human life."[69]

66. *TMS*, 109–13.
67. Raphael and Macfie, "Introduction," 15.
68. Griswold, *Virtues of Enlightenment*, 131.
69. *TMS*, 158.

This phenomenology of moral sentiments works, and this respect for others' opinions and judgments is effective in adjudicating and thus steering morality, because "the all-wise Author of Nature" has taught humans mutual respect and to delight in praiseworthiness while shrinking back from blameworthiness. In this way, explains Smith, humanity is itself "the immediate judge of mankind," having been created "in this respect, as in many others" after the image of this Author. But further, humans must appeal to a much higher tribunal, "to the tribunal of their own consciences, to that of the supposed impartial and well-informed spectator, to that of the man within the breast, the great judge and arbiter of their conduct." Finally, however, when humans' moral judgment fails, and conscience cannot correct, "the only effectual consolation of humbled and afflicted man lies in an appeal to a still higher tribunal, to that of the all-seeing Judge of the world, whose eye can never be deceived, and whose judgments can never be perverted [and who judges with] unerring rectitude."[70] Thus, while the Author has devolved to humanity the responsibility of self-governance through mutual superintendence of virtuous and just conduct, God himself is the final and ultimate judge of moral behavior.

With these conceptual mainstays of Adam Smith's moral philosophy in place, it remains to assess his social theory through the prism of Reformed Christian thought.

## Christian Theistic Evaluation

No doubt there is much in Adam Smith's ethical system that will have resonated favorably with the Reformed Christian reader. Much of his teaching, probably entirely unintentionally, has clear theological integrity, which is unsurprising because he, too, is a creature created in the image of God and as such, at the very least,

70. *TMS*, 128–32.

has access to both general revelation—which includes an analytical view of both history and anthropology—and common grace. Particularly his observations on, and critical analysis of, human nature, from a nontheological perspective, of course, are amazingly acute. Yet he fails to understand what ails humanity, and thus his system is misguided from its point of departure.

We will take a quick look at Smith's broader methodological commitments, with which this chapter opened, and then review the themes and the interpretative value imputed to them by this metaphysical structure. This will be followed by a more precise perspectival examination of Smith's moral system through the analytical framework of the Christian-theistic ethical model as pioneered by Cornelius Van Til. But we will begin with a brief review of the Reformed theological *loci communes* as these appear in standard works of theology by thoroughgoing Reformed stalwarts, convinced as we are of the value of these reminders for a perspectival exercise such as this.

## Reformed Review: Foundational Principles, the Source of Morality

Because God transcends the created order, there is a huge chasm between the Creator and his creatures. There is an absolute ontological difference between an eternal being and a created one. This distinction is best articulated in the attributes (the intrinsic qualities) of God that constitute and coinhere in his very being and demonstrate his qualitative difference from humanity. He has attributes without which he would not be God and which therefore belong to him necessarily and not contingently.

But our Creator is immanent within his creation as well. He is present, active, involved with the created order, and intimately involved with the crowning glory of his creation: humanity. This implies his close superintendence over all things, large and small, as he preserves and providentially guides an unfolding created order to its final consummation.

Humanity being created in the image of God means that there are aspects or qualities of his being—his "communicable" attributes —that he shares with humanity in its pre-fallen state. Choosing disobedience over obedience, humanity embarked on a different path than God had intended for it and now finds itself living with the results: separation from the loving Creator. This sin is an inherent part of being human; all that men and women do, think, and say is always imperfect because somehow touched by sin, and therefore they are incapable of returning to their original state of righteousness without divine intervention. This intervention comes by way of a second chance, freely given. A "covenant of grace" is sovereignly established, in which the person and work of Jesus Christ are central. Although it is monopleuric from the divine perspective (a unilateral, one-sided divine enactment that is unconditional), it is dipleuric from the human side (a bilateral, two-party agreement that is conditional and carries mutual obligations).[71] The human obligation is to appropriate the person and work of Christ by faith and obedience and be restored to a right relationship with God, who desires his (fallen) creatures to conform, in increasing degree, to his image and likeness. Because God shared his "communicable" attributes with humanity at creation, humans can come, by grace, to be better image bearers—to be more ardent in their representation of God.

Humans can decipher God's powerful and glorious being and perfect will through his self-disclosure furnished by way of general

71. This description of covenant theology draws from, among others, Ligon Duncan, "Berkhof on the Nature of the Biblical Concept of Covenant," July 14, 2019, at https://ligonduncan.com/berkhof-on-the-nature-of-the-biblical-concept-of-covenant/. Duncan presents the work of numerous Reformed theologians, in which Louis Berkhof's *Systematic Theology*, 4th ed. (Grand Rapids: Eerdmans, 1941), 262–64, takes center stage.

and special revelation. By the former, God's existence and power can be clearly seen through observing the universe, including the created natural order, the providential progression of history, and the moral and spiritual sensibilities of humanity itself. This disclosure is evident to all of humanity. Special revelation, on the other hand, is not accessible by all, but reserved only for particular men and women, coming at specific times, and distinct places. The Scriptures are the source of such self-disclosure through various modalities: the recording of specific historical events, of God's communication to humanity (through various forms) and, most importantly, of the incarnation itself.[72]

Central to God's self-disclosure is his requirement that humanity should stay true to its covenantal obligations by faithfully pursuing the moral behavior specifically articulated in the Old Testament moral code, but then lifted to another whole (spiritual) level by Jesus Christ in the New Testament. Humans have some capacity to seek to be more like God by faithfully adhering to the behavioral prescriptions (and related proscriptions) that make up this moral code. This is what it means to be holy—to be set apart or consecrated to the glory of God—and this is accomplished through perfect moral living, summarized by Jesus as loving God and neighbor. Such perfection is incomplete until Christians are ushered into the presence of God, but that is no reason to lose hope. Rather, people are exhorted to "be holy yourselves also in all your behavior; because it is written, 'You shall be holy, for I am holy.'"[73] In this fashion is humanity engaged in the project of divine image restoration by aligning with the foundational principles of morality found in the Scriptures. It is a divinely ordained and commanded project of kingdom restoration.

72. Berkhof, *Systematic Theology*, 34–35; Millard J. Erickson, *Christian Theology*, 2nd ed. (Grand Rapids: Baker Academic, 2002), 177–224.

73. In 1 Peter 1:13–16, the apostle reminds us of this command by referring to Leviticus 11:44; 19:2.

## Adam Smith: Phenomenology and Moral Theory

How do the philosophical commitments embedded in Adam Smith's metaphysical, epistemological, and ethical apparatus compare with the foregoing Reformed summary and inform our assessment of these underpinnings of his moral philosophy?

Recognizing from the outset that people are fundamentally social creatures compels Smith to pursue the goal of creating an ideal and flourishing society whose defining characteristic is virtue: "the proper government and direction of all our affections."[74] Smith's ideal world is one where "perfect prudence," "strict justice," and "proper benevolence" are practiced, but are necessarily supported by "the most perfect self-command" to enable the faithful performance of duty.[75] Such a world would thus require some system or code to regulate human behavior. For Smith, a code comprised of "general rules" is not at all what we envision when we consider the regulation of human conduct. Rather, Smith prescribes a universal system of morality comprised of general conformity to socially approved standards of behavior, a behavioral code developed from individuals' judgments of each other. His moral theory is thus built upon observed social interaction that gives rise to ordinary moral judgments, rather than from a philosophical vantage point that prescribes absolute rules based upon, say, eternally divine principles. To construct a moral system in such a bottom-up fashion indicates, among other things, Smith's strong faith in the soundness of judgments made by regular human beings. This phenomenological approach to morality Smith privileges over a top-down method grounded

74. *TMS*, 266. Smith is reviewing three different accounts of the nature of virtue: the systems of Plato, Aristotle, and Xeno, founder of the "Stoical doctrine." In these accounts, virtue consists, respectively, in propriety, prudence, or (disinterested) benevolence (*TMS*, 266–306).

75. *TMS*, 237.

in foundational principles and abiding rules that Smith would consider reductionistic.[76] Because he held that our moral ideas and actions are due to our constitution as social creatures, Smith maintained that our moral action is much better explained by social psychology than by foundational rules of ethics or norms.[77]

In line with this anti-foundational view of moral philosophy, Smith (with Francis Hutcheson and David Hume) was suspicious of the value of reason in determining motive. While reason was crucial in judging the usefulness (or utilitarian promise) of particular character traits revealed in a person's motivation and conduct, it was deemed subordinate to experience, which revealed the ethical character—the intentions—behind that behavior.[78] This is because the capacity to reason is compromised by self-deceit, that "fatal weakness of mankind."[79] But Nature has remedied this weakness and rescued us from the "delusions of self-love" through a continued process of observing the conduct of others, which invariably, almost imperceptibly, will "lead us to form to ourselves certain general rules concerning what is fit and proper either to be done or to be avoided."[80] What's more, when all others agree with our assessment, a body of rules is formed.

> [The general rules of morality] are ultimately founded upon experience of what, in particular instances, our moral faculties, our natural sense of merit and propriety, approve, or

76. For the deeper philosophical insights of *TMS*, I am greatly helped by Fleischacker, "Smith's Moral and Political Philosophy," 1–16.

77. My use of the category "foundational rules" has reference to scriptural (moral) absolutes and is not to be confused with the philosophy of foundationalism. For an accessible summary of Nicholas Wolterstorff's views on foundationalism in relation to the Bible, see Shane Lems, "The Bible and Foundationalism," May 12, 2009, https://reformedreader.wordpress.com/2009/05/12/the-bible-and-foundationalism/.

78. Observations made by Fleischacker, *Philosophical Companion*, 47.

79. *TMS*, 158.

80. *TMS*, 159.

> disapprove of. We do not originally approve or condemn particular actions; because, upon examination, they appear to be agreeable or inconsistent with a certain general rule. The general rule, on the contrary, is formed, by finding from experience, that all actions of a certain kind, or circumstanced in a certain manner, are approved or disapproved of.[81]

Murder, for example, came to be proscribed when the original witness to a murder was personally revulsed by the crime entirely "antecedent to his having formed to himself any such general rule" not to take someone's life.[82] One knows murder to be wrong by witnessing such a detestable crime, not because of some transcendent rule forbidding it. These general rules of conduct, so formulated, go far in countering human conduct driven by excessive self-love.

As crucial as those precepts that make up a virtuous society —prudence, justice, benevolence, and self-command—are to Smith, one searches in vain for some standard of "natural justice" that would facilitate his model of civil society.[83]

And yet, justice is the "main pillar" upholding the "edifice" of society.[84] How helpful it would be to have some standard of "natural justice" showing, for example, the unjustness of society's laws and institutions, and, even more generally, protecting the weak and vulnerable. Smith's moral views, however, make this difficult. In particular, the relative nature of his "general rules," as these differ from one social group to another, make it impossible to develop an absolute, referential system of law. Smith's social theory is time-and-place variable. The harm imposed by injurious infliction upon a person in one society may not be so judged in another. In sum:

81. *TMS*, 159.
82. *TMS*, 159–60.
83. Noted by Fleischacker, *Philosophical Companion*, 46–47.
84. *TMS*, 86; Fleischacker, *Philosophical Companion*, 152.

"No appeal to the natural pungency of pain, or of sympathy with pain, can enable Smith to develop [general principles entrenched in law applicable for all nations]."[85]

We have seen that Smith arrives at moral rules by observing particulars. Therefore, morality is not driven, in the first instance, by the application of a rule, but through the sympathetic spectatorial observance, either approvingly or disapprovingly, of an agent or his actions in a particular context.[86] Via an interesting spectatorial dialectic, we learn to judge others by observing their judgment of us.

Smith's prescription for the fashioning of a virtuous society is based upon contextual personal experience and spectatorial and sympathetic assessment of moral intentions and behavior in a dynamic environment where social values, customs, institutions, and general rules of morality are, to a greater or lesser degree, always in flux. No standard of moral rules constructed in this fashion can have general applicability across all space and time. In the above example, the socially relative structure of injury is obvious. What are the pleasures and pains that receive approval and disapproval in one society as compared to another? That depends on the interpretation of what constitutes "harm." In this instance, how can an impartial spectator enter into, and sympathetically assess, the moral response to pleasure or pain typically approved or disapproved in society at large? The impartial spectator must first know the pleasures and pains typically approved or disapproved in each society, and that society's assessment of harm, before he can be of any use in entering sympathetically into the agent's situation.[87] It can be concluded that Smith's commitment to the evolution of his ethical theory in *TMS* as space-, time-,

85. Fleischacker, *Philosophical Companion*, 158.

86. Griswold, *Virtues of Enlightenment*, 186.

87. And remember, the impartial spectator also goes through this sympathetic process in his self-evaluation.

and people-bound makes the construction of a system of natural justice extremely difficult. Fleischacker comments:

> TMS links the function of morality so closely to the maintenance of society, and makes so much room, accordingly, for the legitimacy of social and historical variation in the way the moral sentiments play themselves out, that it is odd to see Smith writing at all of "general principles which ought to run through and be the foundation of the laws of all nations" (TMS, 341). The whole notion of "natural jurisprudence" is an anomalous one in the context of a moral philosophy like Smith's.[88]

This creates tensions that are irreconcilable. Nowhere in *TMS* is Smith able to articulate general, unchanging principles of justice that might be derived from moral notions.[89] As scholars have observed, Smith's arguments are not based on religious premises. Nor does virtue require religious belief, even though the latter has an important role to play in morality, our moral sentiments being "the vice regents of God within us."[90]

While there is much of value in Smith's phenomenological account of moral theory, it is fundamentally wrongheaded because it introduces a high degree of relativism to his social project of forging a virtuous society. Further, among much else, Smith's civilizing project presupposes much too high a view of human capacity and ability, while ignoring altogether the incapacity resulting from sin. The view of God, humanity, and the created order associated with his deist and Stoic commitments leaves us scrambling for moral certainty and longing for a notion of the good that is capable of underwriting moral lament and hope for a better world.

88. Fleischacker, *Philosophical Companion*, 147, quoting *TMS*, 341.

89. Fleischacker, *Philosophical Companion*, 147, agreeing with Griswold, *Virtues of Enlightenment*, 257.

90. Fleischacker, *Philosophical Companion*, 70, quoting *TMS*, 165–66.

## Adam Smith under Christian-Theistic Scrutiny

Our further analysis of Smith's moral philosophy will be conducted through the grid of the Christian-theistic ethical apparatus developed by Cornelius Van Til.[91] Van Til's system flows from the metanarrative of Scripture—creation, fall, redemption, and consummation—which in turn presupposes a linear view of history. The biblical ethic is a teleological one, where everything moves divinely to its end.

### Goal: Chief Good

The Christian theist considers the goal of the ethical life—the *summum bonum*—to be the consummated kingdom of God, ushered in with the return of Christ and constituted of all the perfections of God's being. Because of its innate teleological orientation, this absolute ethical ideal is a present but anticipatory reality for the people of God, and, in fact, has been so through the entire history of redemption.[92] Christian theistic ethics is therefore an ethics of hope. While the redemptive *summum bonum* is a future reality, however, admission to this perfect ideal occurs in the present through participation in the person and work of Jesus Christ. Inhabitants of this glorious kingdom are thus made righteous by regeneration, are holy, and are blessed. Central to this kingdom-building mission is the complete eradication of

91. Cornelius Van Til, *Christian Theistic Ethics* (Phillipsburg, NJ: Presbyterian and Reformed, 1980). See also John Frame, *The Doctrine of God* (Phillipsburg, NJ: P&R Publishing, 2002), particularly chapters 10–12, where Frame casts Reformed Christian philosophy—ethics, epistemology, metaphysics—within a theology of lordship. On pages 186–87, he explains the topical sequence this way: "The covenantal worldview of Scripture encourages us to see lordship as an ethical relationship that has epistemological and metaphysical implications."

92. Van Til, *Christian Theistic Ethics*, 120–21, drawing from Geerhardus Vos's classic *The Teaching of Jesus concerning the Kingdom of God and the Church* (New York: American Tract Society, 1903), available in multiple reprints and edited editions.

evil, eliminating all that does not reflect God's perfect character and that is not singularly focused on the glory of God and love of neighbor. The motivating power to stay the course, to forge the human will to do the will of God in this honorable endeavor, is true faith. Faith, hope, and love are the theological virtues that constitute the necessary and sufficient conditions for the realization of the kingdom of God. Finally, this realization of the kingdom of God is itself a gift of unmerited, sovereign grace.[93]

Adam Smith's civilizing project has happiness as its ultimate goal, understood in a very Aristotelian and Stoic fashion as a balance between the tranquility and the enjoyment yielded by a virtuous and just society.[94] To his rhetorical question, "What can be added to the happiness of the man who is in health, who is out of debt, and has a clear conscience?"[95] Smith responds: "The chief part of human happiness arises from the consciousness of being beloved,"[96] since "the happiness of mankind . . . seems to have been the original purpose intended by the Author of Nature."[97]

However, with its focus on righteousness as central to the goal of ethical endeavor, Christian-theistic ethics is differently oriented, since it takes seriously humanity's pre-fall and post-fall state. Originally it was inconceivable to imagine a world where there was a contrast between righteousness and happiness, while in our fallen world the righteous fill up the suffering of Christ as they await the restoration of all things, when the new order will once again restore the ideal condition of humanity as created, where righteousness and happiness coinhere in the true and authentic self.[98]

93. Van Til, *Christian Theistic Ethics*, 138–53.
94. *TMS*, 149.
95. *TMS*, 45.
96. *TMS*, 41.
97. *TMS*, 166.
98. Van Til, *Christian Theistic Ethics*, 55.

In stark contrast, Smith's new order is simply an improvement upon that which presently exists. It is merely a hoped for, nonguaranteed, quantitative amelioration of the social and moral health of humanity, effected by the medicine of social improvement as prescribed by the spectatorial process. But this turns out to be a dialectical codification of nonbinding moral agreements without a principled moral context. It is Van Til's man made of water trying to climb out of the water on a ladder made of water.[99]

What is required, rather, is divine surgery by the Great Physician: a heart of flesh must replace the heart of stone. The Reformed Christian's *summum bonum* is thus a qualitatively different one. Smith takes no account of the fallenness of humanity and its inability to move unhampered toward the ideal ultimate end. There is no sin, no need for redemption, and no definitive and progressive sanctification. In Smith's moral theory, a self-determinate, free, unbound, and noncontingent humanity—in other words, humanity as god—exercises ultimate freedom in the building of a just and virtuous society with no transcendent referent.

### Standard

To the Christian theist, humanity is not left without a guide by which it can aspire to accomplish the will of God in movement toward the ideal kingdom. This is his self-revelation spoken of earlier—the standard by which moral behavior is measured and ultimately judged. But the moral law, inscripturated at Sinai, was already part of human nature by virtue of the *imago dei*. Thus, "by nature" men and women have sufficient revelation—"natural law"—to indict them. Closely attending to the apostle Paul's teaching in Romans 2:14–15, John Calvin says that "the purpose of natural law . . . is to render man inexcusable. . . . Natural law is that apprehension of the conscience

99. Cornelius Van Til, *The Defense of the Faith*, 3rd ed. (Phillipsburg, NJ: Presbyterian and Reformed, 1967), 102.

which distinguishes sufficiently between just and unjust, and which deprives men of the excuse of ignorance, while it proves them guilty by their own testimony."[100] All people have an innate sense of moral rectitude to which their consciences testify and which immediately makes them subject to God's righteous judgment.

Yet there is a secondary use of natural law for Calvin: it facilitates the possibility of those non-Christian human societies to which some measure of justice is important.[101] And yet, as Jennifer A. Herdt wisely cautions, "while a Reformed conception of natural law can undergird a general willingness to take part in public moral discourse aimed at constructing a just civic order, it should not be seen as a source of substantive action-guiding moral norms."[102] These are found in the Decalogue, the Christian-theistic directive to living the ethical life. The revelation of this moral standard and the capacity to faithfully live up to its standards as a personal code of conduct are a gift of grace appropriated by faith.

Adam Smith's aversion to foundational rules, laws, and "commands" leaves him with no real guide, no standard for moral behavior. The Decalogue acts neither as a taskmaster to bring sinners to Christ nor as a guide for the ethical and moral life of the redeemed. Smith's system of moral philosophy, anthropocentric to the core, assumes an autonomous moral consciousness, operating through highly interactive social relationships, as the compelling power and ultimate guide for moral behavior. But, in reality, this consciousness can be no more than the immediate or proximate source of information on ethical problems.

The Reformed Christian, on the other hand, recognizing the contingent nature of fallen humanity, clings to the revealed will

100. John Calvin, *Institutes of the Christian Religion*, ed. John T. McNeill, trans. Ford Lewis Battles (Philadelphia: Westminster Press, 1960), 282.

101. See Jennifer A. Herdt, "Calvin's Legacy for Contemporary Reformed Natural Law," *Scottish Journal of Theology* 67, no. 4 (2014): 414–35.

102. Herdt, "Calvin's Legacy," 414.

of God, aware that his spiritually crippled moral consciousness requires this transcendent navigational compass to recognize and then exercise honorable principles of conduct. The self-contained ontological Trinity is the ultimate reference point in all ethical behavior, the ultimate category of interpretation. The moral verdict of any person must be tested by Scripture.[103]

Indeed, the impartial spectator makes mistakes due to excessive self-interest, lack of self-command, self-deception, hypocrisy, poor and distorted judgment, partiality, and more. The central role played by the imagination and conscience in the crucial spectatorial exercise that lies at the center of moral assessment, in Smith's system, is similarly compromised by our inability to freely and truly exercise those constituents of our humanity in its pre-fall integrity. Smith's phenomenologically driven moral philosophy and his commitment to natural religion leave him with no real choice but to seek true justice from that final tribunal, which is, for him, the Author of Nature and the Judge of natural religion.

## Conscience

Similarly, the integrity of the conscience must come under examination. Because of sin, common sense is often faulty in its perceptive capabilities and inaccurate in its read. Consequently, the conscience is misinformed. For Smith, a sense of conscience (and duty) is developed over time—it is part of one's moral education, the development of a moral faculty.[104] Conscience resembles the demigods—partly mortal and partly immortal.[105] For Smith, conscience is entirely noncontingent and self-referential: "It is a function of the actor's own projective and sympathetic imagination

103. Van Til, *Christian Theistic Ethics,* 18–32.
104. Griswold, *Virtues of Enlightenment,* 214.
105. *TMS,* 131.

and thus is fundamentally a matter of the self's relation to self."[106] Such a conception of humanity's autonomy and idolatry of self stands in stark contrast to how conscience was understood by the Reformed orthodox just over a century prior to Smith. Conscience is a divine gift: "The conscience of man . . . is a mans judgement of himself, *according to the judgement of God* of him."[107] Because this judgment presupposes an already "firm and settled" truth, it is practically, not contemplatively, oriented and applies this truth immediately to the active situation with a view to legislating the volition to obedience.[108] This act of practical judgment proceeds by way of the Aristotelian practical syllogism, a helpful heuristic that takes the subject through the standard three steps of adjudication: major premise (biblical law), minor premise (one's behavior), and conclusion (adjudication of that moral conduct). Conscience is constrained and judged by the revealed will of God, his law, as found in the "principles of nature" and in the Scriptures, which demand a person's obedient duty.[109] It is not bound by the laws of the creature.

This developing seventeenth-century moral theology constructed by post-Reformation divines is theocentric to the core, even if it borrows a little too freely from Aristotle. The underlying assumptions of this Puritan and Reformed adjudicatory system regarding the moral life lie well beyond the pale of Adam Smith's metaphysic and epistemology, so foreign are they to eighteenth-century Enlightenment thought. Smith considered the moral struggle to be a genuine part of human existence since impartiality is, at best, an illusion. The natural person is overcome by

106. Griswold, *Virtues of Enlightenment*, 134.

107. William Ames, *Conscience with the Power and Cases Thereof. Devided into V. Bookes* (1639; repr., Norwood, NJ: Walter J. Johnson, 1975), bk. 1, chap. 1, preamble (emphasis added).

108. Jan van Vliet, *The Rise of Reformed System: The Intellectual Heritage of William Ames* (Eugene, OR: Wipf & Stock, 2013), 115.

109. van Vliet, *Reformed System*, 115–19.

self-deceit, rooted in excessive self-love, vanity, and deficient self-command. Smith favored "general rules" to address the weak human condition,[110] even as he searched in vain to uncover them. He scorned the high degree of moral precision required of a life regulated according to a prescribed set of detailed laws of casuistry. He took the side of the ancient moralists, who rejected such "frivolous accuracy" with its "abstruse and metaphysical distinctions," seeking rather to be content with the nurture of "the sentiment upon which justice, modesty, and veracity are founded." Smith opted for ethics and jurisprudence as the "two useful parts of moral philosophy," rejecting casuistry outright.[111] He maintained that moral rules cannot be absolutized by revealed religion and its institutional structures since moral behavior, regulated by laws claiming divine origin and sanction, frequently degenerates into "erroneous conscience," "fanaticism," or worse. Religion itself, then, becomes culpable for the corruption of norms—"the rules ossify into a formula or method for moral assessment." To live in submission to such strict rules of divine authority amounts to hypocrisy.[112] Rather, let the integrity of conduct be driven and adjudicated by the cardinal virtues of prudence, justice, temperance, and fortitude.[113] But this system of virtue ethics requires the generous exercise of self-command since that facilitates a dampening of selfish drives, a modulation of self-interest, and the joyful practice of benevolence.[114] Aristotle simplified this taxonomy of virtue even further by claiming that it "consists in the habit of mediocrity according to right reason. Every particular virtue, according to him, lies in a kind of middle

110. *TMS*, 158–59, 115. Griswold observes that "moral blindness is . . . a major theme in Smith's vivid depiction of moral experience" (*Virtues of Enlightenment*, 134).

111. *TMS*, 340.

112. Griswold, *Virtues of Enlightenment*, 194–96; *TMS*, 171–77, 333–34.

113. *TMS*, 270–71.

114. *TMS*, 215, 237, 241, 262–63, 269.

between two opposite vices."[115] But where does enablement to live virtuously come from? Personifying nature by attributing to it human sensibilities and attributes and then appealing to that nature's deity, its divine authorship, and its providential, universal superintendence, oblige Adam Smith to attribute conscious intentions to it as well. Thus, it is understood that nature enables everyone to live virtuously and exercise the benevolent behavior required of people living in society.

But how is such a world guaranteed and even enforced without some guiding principles of conduct? Systems of virtue ethics are, in the main, constructed on biblical principles. Yet they leave so much to be desired in their exhaustiveness and precision. A Christian moral philosophy presupposes a much superior ideal of humanity than the Aristotelian middle-of-the-roader. "The doctrine of the mean of Aristotle is basically a denial of the idea of the possibility of a perfect man. . . . The whole of ethical endeavor becomes a matter of metaphysical tight-rope walking."[116] A view of humanity that restores it to the crowning glory of God's original creation will obviate the fanciful, speculative philosophies regarding humanity and its conduct delivered to us by the wisdom of the world.

## Summary Observations

The Reformed Christian response to the dilemma posed by the moral philosophy of Adam Smith is, of course, to invoke a holistic theology proper—God as self-sufficient and self-interpreted being, in whom being and consciousness are coterminous. Concomitantly, we must maintain a theological anthropology comprising the created and derived, and then fallen, essence of humanity with an

115. *TMS*, 270, quoting Aristotle, *Nicomachean Ethics*, II.vi.i5, 1106b–7a.

116. Van Til, *Christian Theistic Ethics*, 68–69.

associated epistemology that takes seriously the noetic effects of sin and the consequent failure to see reality as it truly and objectively is. Humans were created perfect, and it is in perfection that they will inhabit the chief good—the realized kingdom of God. But for now, the *imago dei* is a mere shadow of itself, with its debilitating impact on human epistemic and moral endeavor.

Smith's epistemological commitments, however, run closest to the commonsense realism of his successor at Glasgow, Thomas Reid. Smith always privileges the views that come to humans "by nature," including the judgments of ordinary people, over the predications delivered to us by philosophers, intellectuals, and policymakers. He is an immanent critic of humanity's ordinary beliefs, not a transcendent one, since he attempts to correct mistaken beliefs within the rational context of ordinary life, rather than from some elevated standpoint. Commonsense philosophy suits an empirical epistemology well, since it is "fluidly self-corrective," quick in its response to empirical data that Smith processes through interpretation or judgment, rather than observation.[117] But even as a critic of rationalism he overstates humanity's power of reason and perceptive capabilities, assuming as it does neutrality and objectivity. For all facts and events come to us through interpretation and bias, which explains the ultimate foolhardiness of the entire interactive spectatorial process involving agent and impartial spectator. Humanity, either individually or collectively, cannot be the ultimate interpreter of the facts, events, and states of mind that constitute moral behavior, and thus is in no position to adjudicate. Neither humanity created in the image of the "all-wise Author of Nature," nor the "man within the breast," nor Jupiter, nor any other conception of the god of natural religion, can accomplish, ultimately, what only the Christian God can.

117. These luminous insights come from Fleischacker, *Philosophical Companion*, 26–31, 43.

The inherently social nature of humanity has been a foundational pillar of people's forays into anthropological investigation since time immemorial. The conviction that people are social to the core was held by Aristotle over two millennia before Smith. That humans are created in relationship is one of the earliest scriptural teachings, a central premise in theological anthropology. It is a defining truth embedded in humanity's createdness and self-consciousness. This too is Adam Smith's anthropological conviction; he had a highly attuned social conception of self. "All the members of human society stand in need of each others assistance, and are likewise exposed to mutual injuries," he declares. He asserts further that "society flourishes and is happy" when love, gratitude, friendship, and esteem motivate reciprocity of kindness and assistance.[118] But he stops far short of the fuller biblical teaching that has humanity created in, and then fallen out of, a four-way relationship—with God, with self, with others, and with the creation (environment)—necessitating the need for special grace.

The doctrine of grace, so central to a holistic, comprehensive, Christian-theist ethic, is entirely absent from Adam Smith because of his radical metaphysic and epistemology. The many biblical allusions in his observations on humanity and on men and women's personal and social situatedness are testimony to his sophisticated awareness of the Christian metaphysic, even though he does not personally subscribe to it. These strengths Smith exploited to the fullest in building his moral theory. In that respect, Smith's much appealed to "Author of Nature" was generous in showering him with such magnanimous endowments of general revelation and common grace. He is tremendously well-versed in Scripture and has uncommon insights into anthropology, coupled with remarkable psychological intuition.

118. *TMS*, 85.

But Smith's project to construct a moral philosophy ultimately fails to meet the requirements of a normative moral theory. His system falters on its metaphysical and epistemological foundations. His commitment to a particularistic empiricism and his emphasis on contextual knowledge oblige him to build a relativistic moral philosophy to match his evolutionary theory of society. The impartial spectator is constructed within humanity itself from attitudes in the society around it. It is a moral philosophy based entirely on feeling. His phenomenologically determined ethical standards, combined with his antipathy toward foundationalism and his emphasis on contextual knowledge, result in cultural variation in the ethical formulations of his moral philosophy. Smith's work in moral theory has left us with no coherent model of normative morality across all time and space.

The transcendence of ethics demands a universal, foundational system. The Christian-theistic system of ethics adjures principles of conduct grounded in the moral absolutes of the character of God. The principal objective of this moral system is a restoration of original righteousness and happiness, a renewed and perfect state of being toward which history is inexorably advancing. To be part of that redemptive kingdom plan of both striving for and then grasping the chief good—the realization of the kingdom of God on earth—necessitates enabling grace found only in the person and substitutionary, atoning work of Jesus Christ.[119] This grants humans power outside of themselves to reach for the prize. And this grace is appropriated by faith, which becomes the motivating power in the Christian ethical life. Like his silence on grace, Smith has nothing to say about faith.

As we reflect on Smith's insights in moral theory and ethics briefly outlined in this chapter, it would be hard to disagree with

119. Notably, the heavy redaction in the sixth and last edition of *TMS* addresses the substitutionary atonement of Jesus Christ as payment for "our manifold transgressions and iniquities" (*TMS*, nn. 91–92, 383ff.).

the remark that, while Adam Smith is known primarily as the "father of economics," he could lay equal claim to being the "father of sociology."[120] While the next chapter concentrates on what is generally considered to be Adam Smith's magnum opus, recall that he himself considered his moral philosophy to be the much more significant work.

120. Jesse Norman, "Why David Hume and Adam Smith Were the Original Odd Couple: The Engines of the Enlightenment," *Prospect*, September 2017, https://www.prospectmagazine.co.uk/magazine/david-hume-adam-smith-odd-couple.

# 4

# THE INTERPLAY OF HUMANS AND COMMERCIAL SOCIETY

Despite being nearly three times the size of *TMS*, Adam Smith's discourse on political philosophy remains incomplete.[1] He articulated a desideratum for this project as early as the first edition of *TMS*. In the last two lines of that work, he discloses his plan to produce a comprehensive account of the history of jurisprudence, including "the general principles of law and government" within a social-historical evolutionary framework, which would

1. This introductory section draws on material from Samuel Fleischacker, "Adam Smith's Moral and Political Philosophy," *Stanford Encyclopedia of Philosophy* (November 11, 2020), https://plato.stanford.edu/entries/smith-moral-political/#SumSmiMor; Fleischacker, *On Adam Smith's* Wealth of Nations*: A Philosophical Companion* (Princeton, NJ: Princeton University Press, 2005); Jack Russell Weinstein, "Adam Smith (1723–1790)," *Internet Encyclopedia of Philosophy*, https://iep.utm.edu/smith/; Andrew Skinner, "Introduction," in *The Wealth of Nations, Books I-III*, ed. Skinner (New York: Penguin Books, 1979), 11–97; Robert L. Heilbroner, "Adam Smith: Scottish Philosopher," March 7, 2024, https://www.britannica.com/biography/Adam-Smith; D. D. Raphael and A. L. Macfie, "Introduction," *TMS*; Jeffrey T. Young, "Andrew Skinner, the Glasgow Edition, and Adam Smith," *Œconomia* 2–3 (2012): 365–76; R. H. Campbell and A. S. Skinner, "General Introduction," *WN*, 1–60.

include accounts of justice, police (public policy), revenue, arms, "and whatever else is the object of law."[2] This would be the first such attempt since the landmark work of Hugo Grotius (1583–1645), says Smith. Thirty-one years later, circling back to this 1759 statement in an "Advertisement" that introduced the sixth and final edition of *TMS,* Smith acknowledged that this plan was only partially fulfilled in *WN*. What remained missing was the theory of jurisprudence, which he still hoped to produce, having "not altogether abandoned the design."[3] And while elements of his views on jurisprudence and justice appeared in other works, particularly in the student notes that comprise *LJ,* a systematic treatment never materialized, and Smith's desire for a comprehensive, philosophical program remained unfulfilled.

Given Smith's larger vision of his project, and while some may view him as "a philosopher who published less than he promised,"[4] both *TMS* and *WN* constitute individual, yet inseparable, pieces of his grander philosophical consciousness. *WN* only makes sense as a continuation of the philosophical theme commenced in *TMS,* but writ large within commercial society. In the latter work, the ultimate problem that Smith identifies and studies in great detail is a very individual one—the inner struggle between the passions and the impartial spectator. In *WN,* Smith takes this struggle and applies it to the larger stage of history itself—both to the characteristics

2. *TMS,* 342.

3. *TMS,* 3. Griswold gives a detailed and helpful overview of the issue regarding Smith's unfinished corpus. This includes taking his own stated hermeneutical assumptions into "the thickets of Smith's philosophy," searching for clues with which to untangle the issue of the missing theory of jurisprudence—which would include a comprehensive and systematic account of justice—and then suggesting ways in which this incompleteness of Smith's projected work can be explained; see his *Adam Smith and the Virtues of Enlightenment* (Cambridge: Cambridge University Press, 1999), 29–39, 256–58.

4. The assessment of Nicholas Phillipson, "Adam Smith: A Biographer's Reflection," in *The Oxford Handbook of Adam Smith,* ed. Christopher J. Berry, Maria Pia Paganelli, and Craig Smith (Oxford: Oxford University Press, 2013), 24.

contemporaneous to Smith's own time and in the future evolution of society, study of which would uncover the different forms of sociability throughout history. The complementarity of these volumes is obvious and must be seen together as a reification of his systematizing spirit. Adam Smith himself spoke of the beauty of "systematical arrangement."[5] His ethics, jurisprudence, and economics are constructed in such a way as to reveal a great capacity for model building, while properly delineating the boundaries of this single system of which these three interconnected disciplines constitute component parts.[6] Such arrangement is true to both the purpose of philosophy—to explain the coherence of nature—and the recognition of the interdependence of phenomena. "In the manner of Sir Isaac Newton we may lay down certain principles known or proved in the beginning, from whence we account for the severall Phenomena, connecting all together by the same Chain."[7] For Smith, all humanity has this "propensity"—"to account for all appearances from as few principles as possible."[8] Reality only makes sense when understood in systems and patterns.

This is a chief value of both *TMS* and *WN*: even if some of Adam Smith's ideas were not original, he took existing principles and refined the reasoning used in their formulation while scientifically demonstrating their interconnectedness. As such and like *TMS, WN* represents a "great synthetic performance," recounting the state of the art and science of political economy as it evolved in Smith's thinking since the 1760s, but also from that represented by the physiocrats of the day.[9] Building on the ethical foundations earlier laid in *TMS,* and incorporating many ideas proposed in much of his other work, Smith constructed a

5. *WN,* 768–69.
6. Campbell and Skinner cogently illustrate this in "General Introduction," *WN,* 2–5.
7. *LRBL,* 145–46.
8. *TMS,* 299.
9. Campbell and Skinner, "General Introduction," 23.

magnificent edifice of economic thought. This paradigm models the commercial interests of an orderly society from his previously prescribed ethical, psychological, philosophical, and methodological propositions—a construct of political economy that was itself further developed by his successors.

Formally constructing such an impressive system involved first analyzing individual problems (the details)—elements we would today classify within the realm of *microeconomics,* before moving on to *macroeconomics,* which illustrates the mutual connectedness of the elements of the former and the interdependence of the whole. For Smith, this meant elucidating how the largely free market exchange economy operates by employing theoretical building blocks that together comprise the body of theory that constitutes his system.

This body of theory presupposes two fundamental assumptions of a broadly sociological and psychological character which derive their meaning from the nature of humans as social beings. Humanity is found to inhabit both the social state outside of which humans cannot function and a particular social structure wherever the exchange economy dominates. The former constitutes the essence of *TMS* and drives the underlying dynamic of *WN.* How fit is one to inhabit a commercial society and engage with the exchange economy? How do humans balance the selfish and the social? This fitness and balancing act depend on certain "propensities," traits of character, that make for successful engagement in economic interchange. *TMS* is a study of human faculties and propensities granted by the Author of Nature and tempered through social intercourse. Think of the place of sympathy (empathy), imagination, reason, and reflection as these human faculties enable predispositions toward a healthy "fellow feeling"—love for others—and an unhealthy self-love. When applied to economic interchange, such inclinations have potential to reinforce both harmony and disharmony in the social sphere. To avoid the latter, certain sources of control that are well known and observed by all members of society—for example, rules of justice and morality—are needed. The key to social order, then, is the restraint that members of the social arrangement impose upon themselves.

In sum, Smith has created a model of personal and social behavior, at the heart of which are the virtues of prudence, benevolence, justice, and self-command. These attributes of human nature are necessary building blocks in the construction of the ideal community—a commercial society. Individuals socialized in such a fashion not only are prepared for engagement in the exchange economy, but also spur others on to similar behavior and, as such, benefit the state, for a cardinal axiom of political economy is that

> in a certain view of things all the arts, the science(s), law and government, wisdom, and even virtue itself tend all to this one thing, the providing meat, drink, rayment, and lodging for men, which are commonly reckoned the meanest of employments and fit for the pursuit of none but the lowest and meanest of people.[10]

And this is the business of commercial society.

## Thematic Analysis of Smith's Political Economy

*WN* is developed around the central theme that commercial society, left unencumbered, best advances the material well-being of its members in pursuit of their self-interest. Societal prosperity is maximized if prevailing economic forces are left to move freely without the direction or oversight of a central authority such as

10. *LJ(A)*, 338.

the state and other institutions. This was the attraction of the work in 1790 and continues to be the magnetic power of free market political economy today.

Smith articulates his system of economic philosophy in five sequential books that together underscore the interdependence of economic phenomena and the patterns of social relations between groups of economic agents. This work represents the foundation of what has come to be designated as the "classical school" of economics and is the body of work upon which all subsequent economic thought—form and content—is based. Recall that many of the principles had been conceived by earlier representatives of the school with varying degrees of coherence, but they were codified, synthesized, and systematized in *WN*. Before proceeding through Smith's work, it might be helpful to summarize some general features of classical economics, which can then be used as anchors into which the principle elements of Smith's thought can be "hooked" for greater clarity.[11] These features are:

1. Economics is subject to laws to be studied and employed to improve living standards.
2. Society is stratified by social classes whose members have differing roles in the economic process.
3. Much of economic activity is self-regulating and finds "equilibrium" through the coordinated working of independent markets.
4. Economic processes have unintended consequences because self-interested economic agents are fallible, unable

11. I have drawn on many sources in the following explication and analysis of *WN*, including Skinner, "Introduction"; Campbell and Skinner, "General Introduction," *WN*; Jerry Evensky, "The Wealth of Nations," in *Adam Smith: His Life, Thought, and Legacy*, ed. Ryan Patrick Hanley (Princeton, NJ: Princeton University Press, 2016), 67–88; Eamonn Butler, *The Condensed Wealth of Nations and the Incredibly Condensed Theory of Moral Sentiments* ([London:] Adam Smith Institute, 2011), at www.adamsmith.org.

to conceive of the end results of large-scale interdependence and interaction.

5. The wealth of nations is maximized, not by hoarding gold, silver, and other precious metals, but through labor, production, and increasing labor productivity, which results in a surplus product (GDP).
6. Free competition minimizes production costs, resulting in uniform levels of profit and a gravitation of prices to their "natural" level, which is the labor cost of producing it (i.e., the "labor theory of value"). "Market prices" will in the long run gravitate here.
7. A monopolistic spirit, with its characteristic network of privileges and impediments to labor and capital mobility (as characterized by, for example, the feudal system), is stifled by an interdependent market of freely competing agents in which there are no barriers to entry or exit.[12]

## Economic Theory: Wealth Creation, Productivity, Trade, and Value

Commencing from a largely microeconomic, analytical perspective, Adam Smith asserts that the wealth of nations, total income and output, is maximized through the most efficient employment of land, labor, and capital. Today we measure this economic production as Gross Domestic (or National) Product, GDP. Production per person is the central measure that speaks to a society's capacity to produce, and this is optimized by the division of labor whereby each individual worker focuses on one individual task in the production process. Such "specialization of labor" results in greater productivity and improved affluence, which, in a well-governed society, benefits everyone, including the

12. Summarized from Heinz D. Kurz, *Economic Thought: A Brief History*, trans. Jeremiah Riemer (New York: Columbia University Press, 2016), 17–41.

poorest. Central to the success of such a society is the widespread cooperation between all those involved in a productive endeavor. The resulting wealth of such collaborative social networks explains the accumulation of wealth in the more developed economies.[13]

These labor and production efficiencies are themselves the product of individuals' innate drive for material self-improvement, "the natural response to necessity," in accord with an entrepreneurial spirit. This psychology of self-improvement builds on a similar proposition in *TMS,* where Smith explains that one works for personal improvement to receive the approbation of the impartial spectator, and this tenet became the "animating principle" driving human society and civilization's advance.[14] This conjecture broadened in Smith's understanding of humanity to include people's need for each other. But it would be a mistake to assume that others' help comes from an inborn spirit of benevolence, continues Smith: "It is not from the benevolence of the butcher, the brewer, or the baker, that we expect our dinner, but from their regard to their own interest. We address ourselves, not to their humanity but to their self-love."[15] As explained earlier, this statement is the focal point of much Smithian misinterpretation, which would be avoided by heeding Eugene Heath's wise counsel in Smithian hermeneutics: "Adam Smith does not reduce motivation to a single drive. Just as there are plural springs of conduct, so are there various concepts of self-interest, including self-preservation, selfishness, and self-love."[16]

13. *WN,* 13–24.

14. *WN,* 341, and *TMS,* 50–66; Phillipson, "Biographer's Reflection," 32–33.

15. *WN,* 25–27. In *WN* the emphasis on "self-love" reflects a concern for one's own well-being that is entirely natural and necessary for one's own survival. Recall from chapter 3 that concern for the well-being of one's neighbor is a constitutive element in optimizing one's own happiness. For Smith, there is a significant place in human nature for legitimate self-love, which he elsewhere describes as exercising the virtue of "prudence" (*TMS,* 212–17).

16. Eugene Smith, "Adam Smith and Self-Interest," in Berry, Paganelli, and Smith, *Oxford Handbook,* 241.

The material surplus created from ever-rising productivity engendered by the division of labor and specialization gives economic agents occasion to barter and exchange, and that activity is facilitated by money. This latter "invention" obviates the previously necessary and sufficient condition of the "double coincidence of wants," an almost impossible condition to meet in the exchange economy. "Money," says Smith, "has become in all civilized nations the universal instrument of commerce," with the happy consequence of greater production and market expansion. Be clear, though, that this lubricant of economic exchange, while central in facilitating further economic growth, must not be mistaken for wealth.[17] Smith sends out constant reminders of this fact, which somewhat later in his work will be the central rationale for his thoroughgoing critique of mercantilism. Money does not constitute wealth, but it can help create it.

Trade and productivity are commensurate with the size of the market in an exchange economy. Because trade—the "power of exchange"—induces the division of labor and its corollary, heightened productivity, it is logical that the goal of economic enterprise is to increase market size. Facilitating such an "automatic" system is the goal of political economy. Conversely, any encumbrance to such free exchange between economic agents retards economic progress.

The underlying value of a tradable commodity determines its price. That value—the "natural" price—is fundamentally determined by the labor absorbed in its production. Hear Smith: "Labour . . . is the real measure of the exchangeable value of all commodities. . . . The real price of everything, what everything really costs to the man who wants to acquire it, is the toil and trouble of acquiring it." The real wealth we obtain from exchanging

17. *WN*, 27–46. Smith presents a thorough excursus of the origin, evolution, and use of money.

with others is the value of their embodied labor, not their money, which represents the "nominal" price paid because currency is based on the underlying and changing value of the specie. The value of a commodity produced by employing the entire suite of input categories—land, labor, and capital—is likewise determined by calculating their embedded labor equivalencies. The natural price represents the monetary return to producers reflecting their costs of manufacture, while the return to capital is proxied by the interest rate—the cost of borrowing. The natural price could be at variance with the exchange value ("market" price) determined by the volume of goods brought to market compared to the number of potential buyers, and, in fact, it often is. Some ambiguity exists in Smith's postulation that exchange value depends on both the value of labor embedded in its production and also by the labor that a good commands on the market. The two are not the same.[18]

## Economic Theory: Factors of Production and Their Returns

In what is generally considered to be the technically most advanced section of Adam Smith's insights and assertions in *WN* —"perhaps among the best from a purely analytical point of view"[19] —he demonstrates the progressive, self-feeding inertia brought about by continual economic growth to now include, with labor, further acquisition of capital stock and land, and the corresponding returns to these input categories: wages, profits, and rent, respectively. By eighteenth-century standards, this is a fairly complex model of the exchange economy. The increased generation of output and income transforms this economic dynamic into a virtuous circle. More income stimulates purchases, necessitating further production

18. *WN*, 37–81. Karl Marx (1818–83) made his interpretation of Smith's labor theory of value the centerpiece of his Hegelian, conflict-driven process of historical change known as "dialectical materialism."

19. Campbell and Skinner, "General Introduction," 25.

and thus capital deepening. Need arises for constantly increasing pools of labor to mobilize this capital for productive use. More product and profit ensue, the latter reflecting the value of the capital used in the production process, compensating owners of capital for their effort, imagination, and risk taking. Capital deepening lies at the heart of economic progress since this drives the more intensive division of labor, increases the productive capacity of society, and expands the wealth of the nation.[20]

With these determinants of commercial exchange in place, Smith creates a fairly well-developed supply-and-demand model that ensures "market-clearing" conditions as prices move up or down, depending on the fluctuating forces of demand and supply. Oversupply reduces prices and undersupply increases them, as market participants engage and bid prices down or up until markets "clear." Continued overstocking of the market could result in prices falling below the cost of production, triggering a fall in output as the seller withdraws the productive employ of the three input categories, whose returns fall proportionately. Such reduction in supply restores market prices and, with them, production costs, and the bidding process of economic agents again clears the market. The opposite dynamic occurs during market shortages. Notice that these market movements affect the intensity of use of the factors of production. And returns to the three input categories undergo the same dynamic adjustment.[21] One can see how crucial to the smooth, unfettered operation of the market is free and unmanaged exchange.

What Smith has just described is the dynamism of the "self-regulating" nature of the market in an exchange economy. This pivotal market adjustment is in harmony with the emphasis on scarcity and choice described in any number of textbook definitions of the science of economics. A classic description puts it like

20. *WN*, 65–71.
21. *WN*, 72–81, 105–15.

this: "Economics is the study of the allocation of scarce resources amongst competing uses." Resources are scarce and finite, but human wants are infinite. Through competitive forces, these scarce resources (land, labor, capital) gravitate to where they add the most value, a movement purely determined by the price system. The market is an entirely inevitable system, self-adjusting through what some call the workings of the "invisible hand," which, for Smith, refers to the general providentialism of the Author of Nature, or natural theology.[22] Notice that we see both static and dynamic elements in Smith's analysis of market forces. A market price is established when supply and demand meet at a point in time. But over time, with changing economic conditions, the market price adjusts, based upon supply and demand for factors of production and for final goods. Freely determined exchange unlocks the inherent potential in an economy.

The automatic adjustment process imposed by competitive pressures ensures that the net benefits of employing labor and capital equalize across all applications (or uses) despite legitimate wage differentials. Customer satisfaction is the only "real and effective discipline" over businesses and will force wage and price equilibrium in labor and capital markets. The consumer reigns supreme. Any system of market management or interference will result in a less than optimal allocation of labor and capital and will result in power blocks of special interest groups that are not in the general interest of the state.[23]

22. The highly contested meaning of this phrase overlooks its common usage in seventeenth- and eighteenth-century Scotland, where it was used in sermons, plays, poetry, and political rhetoric. Smith uses it a total of only three times in his entire corpus. See my forthcoming "Adam Smith (1723–90): Social Imaginary and Religion," in *Pro Rege*, March 2025.

23. *WN*, 116–59; 160–264. The editors note that the final chapter of Book I (pp. 160–275) is "among the longest and most complex of the whole work" (Campbell and Skinner, "General Introduction," 27). Its length is in part due to a 75-page digression on the changing price of silver over the previous four hundred years.

The interdependence of these "three great, original and constituent orders" of every civilized society—the input categories and those who derive their income from them—all contribute their share to a country's annual produce. It is a marvelous exposition of the interconnectedness of social groups. The interests of landlords and workers coincide with the general interests of society because as general levels of wealth rise, so do wages and rents. Employers, on the contrary, are more concerned with the success of their own enterprise than about advancing the welfare of the state. Adam Smith closes his largely microeconomic exposition of economic structures by advising that any policy or regulatory recommendation coming from this order must always be viewed with suspicion.[24]

### Economic Theory: Capital Accumulation and the Labor Force

Turning his focus to more macroeconomic concerns, Smith notes that just as a rise in returns to labor is occasioned, not by the *level* of national wealth, but by its *increase,* so the *growth* in capital stock improves the material position of investors in capital. As the given stock of capital facilitates an initial division of labor, the resultant improved productively spurs more labor division, further increasing capital stock requirements. "The quantity of industry, therefore, not only increases in every country with the increase of the stock which employs it, but, in consequence of that increase, the same quantity of industry produces a much greater quantity of work."[25] The more that is invested in capital stock, the greater is production efficiency.

Adam Smith's conception of the multiple categories of capital stock sounds foreign to contemporary sensibilities because of

24. *WN*, 264–75.
25. *WN*, 277.

taxonomic differences in macroeconomic classification. But his articulation of fixed capital and its power in economic growth and development is insightful. "Fixed" capital is investment in future productive and income-generating capacity, such as machinery and equipment, buildings, land improvements, and, interestingly, also "employed" livestock and the productive abilities of members of society—the labor force, in contemporary terms. Money is the instrumental, liquefied form that capital assumes to lubricate economic exchange and to render capital stock productive.[26] Smooth operation of this central role requires a competitive, efficient, prudent, and regulated institutional banking system to ensure circumspect conduct on the part of banks, which fulfill a pivotal role in economic development.[27]

Consistent with his central concern that capital accumulation lies at the center of increasing national wealth, Adam Smith now turns to the closely related matter of labor productivity, which both drives and is the product of capital deepening in an unending virtuous circle, the dynamics of which are constitutive of the capital theory of *WN*. His assignment of productive and unproductive endeavor to differing labor groups recalls his time-bound classification of capital stock. But his contribution is most astute in tracing the labor that adds value ("productive") by producing physical commodities yielding revenue. This contrasts with unproductive service-producing labor (of which his working example is that of a "menial servant").[28] Although not always

26. *WN*, 279–86. See also Tony Aspromourgos, "Adam Smith on Labour and Capital," in Berry, Paganelli, and Smith, *Oxford Handbook*, 267–89.

27. *WN*, 287–329. The competitive banking system of eighteenth-century Scotland was "commodity based," compared to the fiat money used today. Banks could issue their own money, which could lead to irresponsible practices. An excellent overview of the banking system of Adam Smith's day is found in Maria Pia Paganelli, "Adam Smith and the History of Economic Thought: The Case of Banking," in Hanley, *Adam Smith: His Life*, 247–61.

28. It is noted that Smith's habitual use of the "menial servant" persona as representative of unproductive labor imputes a certain moral aspect to the distinction

consistent in his definitions, Smith recognizes that the provision of services has value, but these are consumed immediately and are affordable only for the owners of land and capital; this category of labor includes what we would today call the service professions. The problem lies in the fact that there is no reinvestment of this "unproductive" labor in the capital deepening process and, in fact, this process is hampered, since such consumption reduces the savings necessary for capital investment. Scholars suggest that it may be truer to Smith's intentions that by "services" he actually means luxury services, since to some services he ascribes value—just not the kind that yields revenues for reinvestment.[29] Firing a salvo at government workers, Smith claims that "they are themselves always and without any exception, the greatest spendthrifts in the society."[30] Yet, despite government expenditure and mismanagement, the economy moves forward due to the individual's built-in drive for improvement. Leaving commercial activity to the private sector ensures that private individuals will accumulate the savings necessary to facilitate capital deepening.[31]

## Economic Theory: Interest and Capital Employment

The interest rate charged for borrowed money (liquid stock) is, like all other goods, dependent on the competitive forces in the economy, and Smith advises that these funds be channeled into productive capital stock, rather than current expenditures. This perpetuates the dynamic cause-and-effect chain of economic growth and expanded "opulence."[32] Adam Smith prioritizes capital

---

between service-producing and goods-producing endeavors; see Aspromourgos, "Smith on Labour and Capital," 278.

29. For example, see Aspromourgos, "Smith on Labour and Capital," 275–76.

30. *WN*, 346.

31. *WN*, 330–49. The prominence of Smith's capital theory in *WN*, both in its particulars and extensions, is a refining of the macroeconomic work of Turgot and Quesnay of the Physiocrat School; see Aspromourgos, "Smith on Labour and Capital," 276.

32. *WN*, 350–59.

stock by the productivity of its employment, a schema where farm laborers (which group includes cattle and nature) are ranked highest, then manufacturers, and finally wholesale and retail traders, the former of which include foreign traders. He justifies this ranking by indicating the high returns on agricultural investment enjoyed by the American colonies, which imported most manufacturing products while the consumer benefited from lower prices generally across the board. The macroeconomic implications of people's acquisitive, bartering, and trading nature mean that economic progress and a nation's well-being are always improved through international trade.[33]

The articulation of the theory of value and distribution from both a static and a dynamic point of view, as presented in the first two books of *WN*, represents the marrow of Adam Smith's theoretical analytics and expresses a view of political economy that he considers the "natural course of things." Readers will have noticed a "circular flow" dynamic at play in the foregoing analysis, where the theory of price and distribution is coupled with the theory of accumulation of capital, and where personal and corporate income and spending/saving stimulates production and wealth creation. The long-run trends in rates of wages, profits, and rent are driven by the competitive forces of the exchange economy freely at work. Disruption of this natural course by, typically, human institutions, derails the progression of an economy from its original state, and, consequently, short-circuits the "natural progress of opulence." While there is much agreement on the static and dynamic dimensions of Adam Smith's microeconomic contributions and the "circular flow" model of the macroeconomy, the value of his curious three-way division of the labor productivities of capital, and of his upcoming narrative regarding economic development ("Progress of Opulence") based thereon,

33. *WN*, 360–75.

is heavily discounted. No less a Smithian expert than Andrew Skinner regards these as the weakest element in the entire edifice of Adam Smith's political economy.[34]

## Economic History: The Natural Progress of Economic Development and Its Subversion

The thrust of the shortest book in *WN* is to contrast the "natural" progress of economic growth with alternatives arising from impediments retarding development. As a founder of the Scottish School of history, Smith was instrumental in introducing an approach to historical inquiry designated as "philosophical" or "theoretical" and as "natural." The former underscored the analytical purpose of the study, while the latter concentrated on the process of societal development through history, from primitive to advanced. This historiographical approach yielded a theory of economic development and human progress, which held that the natural order of human progress was to move successively through four stages of development: the age of hunters, of shepherds, of agriculture, and of commerce. Each new stage manifested increased need for state oversight primarily to ensure justice.[35]

Based on his threefold ranking of productive endeavor (agriculture, manufacturing, wholesale and retail trade), Smith avers that economic development commences with the interaction

34. Campbell and Skinner, "General Introduction," 32.

35. *LJ(A)*, 14–16, 27–28, 107, 218–21; *LJ(B)*, 459. Not all agree on the value of Smith's historiographical thesis. See, for example, Maria Pia Paganelli, "Adam Smith and Economic Development in Theory and Practice: A Rejection of the Stadial Model?," *Journal of the History of Economic Thought* 44, no. 1 (March 2022): 95–104, at https://doi.org/10.1017/S1053837220000309, and a defense by Jerry Evensky, "Wealth of Nations," 70. Dennis Rasmussen maintains the most probable view, that, on the basis of multiple "exceptions and ambiguities" to this development model mentioned in his other writings, Smith most likely used this theory more as a "loose outline or heuristic device" by which different forms of society are compared (*The Problems and Promise of Commercial Society: Adam Smith's Response to Rousseau* [University Park, PA: Pennsylvania State University Press, 2008], 99–101).

between rural (agriculture) and urban (manufacturing and trade) society—the country and the town. Mutual benefits result from the complementary provision of markets: the country provides raw materials, including food, in exchange for the town's finished products, such as tools and household goods. That's why the North American and West Indian colonies have done so well: they have focused on land development, sent raw materials to England, and depended on the mother country for their finished goods. Unencumbered capital flows first to land development (the "country") and only then to the "town."[36]

The final stage of Smith's natural order represents the most developed period in his "conceptual" or "philosophical" theory of history, within which he provides a two-sector case of commercial relations, manufacturing and agriculture. Although his work is on political economy, Smith has in mind the multiple aspects of human experience in society—political, social, and to a lesser degree the religious—in addition to the strictly economic. These dimensions of human society are very much interrelated, and progress in one area presupposes complementary progress in the others, primarily in the institutions that give concrete shape to the culture's ethos and guiding principles. Smith's proximate goal is to foster the commercial progress of Great Britain, but his ultimate purpose is always to improve the condition of humanity. To convince his audience of his view of the world and the logic of his economic system-building, the narrative often makes long excursions through the history of Europe and other countries in his search for cogent examples and counterexamples from other societies.

His review of history demonstrates just how severely human institutions have inverted this natural order. "This is classic Smith," one scholar observes, to take a "theoretical or conjectural history" that describes the "natural progress of opulence," where laws

36. *WN*, 376–80, 411–27.

and institutions evolve in proper alignment with each successive stage of development, and contrast this with an actual history of entrenched misalignment.[37]

The social chaos engendered by the fall of Rome elevated rich landholding barons to powerful socioeconomic and political positions from whence they exerted arbitrary power. Paradoxically, some degree of order did ensue, advancing the development of urban areas with the concomitant rise in wealth—including landholdings. Townspeople were granted privileges and a degree of self-government as they sided with weak kings in opposition to rich landowning barons who did nothing to improve the rural land and develop it, considering land accumulation exclusively as a source of wealth and power, patronage, and protection. For "it seldom happens . . . that a great proprietor is a great improver." In this medieval period, a feudal system of law was established, with limited success in curbing the arbitrary power of the landowners. With the rise of manufacturing and commerce, landlord power diminished, and a rudimentary system of justice developed. Here Adam Smith returns to a theme that first appeared in his Glasgow lectures of the early 1760s regarding the rising need for government with the evolution of civil society. With civil advance and unevenly rising wealth come mounting power struggles between the rich and the poor and ensuing injustice. Recall that for Smith the chief of all virtues was justice: all jurisprudence was to be established with that outcome in view.[38] This emphasis led to a review of contemporary economic systems that Smith rightly dismissed out of hand.

## Economic Systems: Mercantilism

Mercantilism was based on the theory that a country's wealth is measured by the volume and value of its gold and silver reserves,

37. Evensky, "Wealth of Nations," 77, referring to Smith biographer Dugald Steward's insights on Smith's historiography in *EPS*, 293.

38. *WN*, 381–427.

of which there was only a limited worldwide supply. It was the economic policy dominating eighteenth-century international economic affairs, and while carried out with considerable variation by its principal devotees, powerful England and France, the ruling philosophical principles and associated policy regimes were very similar, and most nation states adopted mercantilism to some degree. It was propelled by the rapid colonization that characterized the age of exploration, and both resulted from, and fueled, imperialism. The relationship between England and its American colonies was watched closely by Adam Smith, who heavily criticized the mercantilist policies that England was imposing on its North American colonial empire. He advised that both parties try to resolve things peaceably, "as good friends," so that the damage done by recent acrimonies would be reversed through a revival of "the natural affection of the colonies to the mother country." Such conciliatory behavior is advisable, said Smith, with some prescience, since the colonial "empire" "seems very likely to become, one of the greatest and most formidable that ever was in the world."[39] Adam Smith considers the American colonies to be the best example of colonial enterprises despite, not because of, mercantilism.[40]

Mercantilism was "one of the great whipping boys in the history of economics,"[41] the "economic version of warfare" at the time of the passage of the feudal system into the geopolitical entity of nation states. The parties involved in a mercantile system are the manufacturers and merchants, whose avarice is supported by heavily lobbied governments in battle with the poor, voiceless consumer. Smith saw this as an enormous conspiracy, where a

39. *WN*, 556–641.

40. *WN*, 540, 614–23.

41. *WN*, 642–62; well described by C. W. London, "What Was Mercantilism?," *The Economist* (August 23, 2013), at https://www.economist.com/free-exchange/2013/08/23/what-was-mercantilism.

country's goal was encouraged by generous and preferential state policy to maximize production for sale to foreign countries, curtail imports for home use and thus discourage consumption, and ignore the economic oppression of the poor, who were expected to live at the margins of subsistence.[42]

The entire goal of mercantilism was to protect national commerce and line a country's coffers with money, the payment received from exports as measured and submitted in gold and other precious metals. This meant maximizing exports (benefiting domestic merchants and manufacturers) and minimizing imports (harming the consumer through much higher prices and shortages of imported goods). Various discriminatory political and economic measures were imposed to discourage imported, particularly manufactured, goods. Further, the colonies were proscribed from conducting international trade with anyone other than the "mother country." Exports of specie were banned to ensure its growing inventory, while production of goods for the export trade received highly preferential treatment. Furthermore, domestic manufacturing and industry were promoted through research or direct subsidies. In this perennial game, the poor remained poor, and the rich became richer. The privileged members of society included government officials, inspectors, judges, and enforcement officers, all directly and indirectly connected to the domestic benefits of mercantilism.[43]

This policy construct of the political economy of the day was underpinned and justified by comprehensive social philosophies that included what we would today consider unthinkable policies and horrendous practices. It was thought that high wages would incline the lower working classes to lives of leisure and the accompanying social ills that would befall society. Thus, remuneration

42. *WN*, 428–51.
43. *WN*, 452–555.

for workers should be maintained at a subsistence wage. Central in discussions on morality and the economic theory of the day were the views of Dutch philosopher and medical doctor Bernard de Mandeville as articulated in his *Fable of the Bees*. He asserted that it was to the great benefit of society to have a "Multitude of laborious Poor," a social class that should be spared from idleness, for "it was Prudence to relieve their wants, but Folly to cure them. . . . To make the Society happy and People easy under the meanest circumstances, it is requisite that great Numbers of them should be Ignorant as well as Poor."[44] If workers were overpaid, children would not need to work. Idle children guaranteed further erosion of a "happy" society. And paying barely subsistence wage ensured all income was spent on "necessaries," thus avoiding opportunity for saving and leisure[45] and, as we have seen, crippling capital deepening and further economic development opportunities through short-circuiting the resource-allocative powers of the price mechanism.

One of Mandeville's central theses was that certain vices, such as vanity and greed, are socially beneficent. He demonstrated that self-interest and the desire for material well-being, commonly stigmatized as vices, are in fact the incentives that make for general welfare, prosperity, and civilization. Pursuit of personal pleasure, exercise of self-interested passions, satisfaction of material desires, serving neighbors only to advance one's own acquisition of wealth: these were among the essential factors and human forces fostering innovation, ingenuity, and industry, the cumulative outcome of which was the vast wealth and wonders of a thriving society. It was the pursuit of self-interest, not benevolence, that advanced society.[46]

44. Bernard Mandeville, *Fable of the Bees*, ed. F. B. Kaye (London: Oxford University Press, 1924), 193–94, 248, 287–88.

45. Phyllis Vandenberg, "Bernard Mandeville (1670–1733)," *Internet Encyclopedia of Philosophy*, https://iep.utm.edu/mandevil/.

46. Vandenberg, "Bernard Mandeville."

Logically, such a system of thought encouraged enterprising minds to adopt related philosophies of society-building with attendant extensions and applications. Policies of child labor was one of these. At four years of age, children should be employed in activities best suited to their abilities—their "age, strength and capacity," advocated William Temple (1628–99) from his socially elevated and politically connected position. They should "earn their living" because there was work aplenty for them, and habits of constant employment "would at length prove agreeable and entertaining to them."[47]

While many of the protectionist policies enacted to reflect the philosophies of contemporary political and economic nationalism are seen in various forms and expressions today in the twenty-first century, the tenets of this system of economic management have had little to no salutary effects on economic policy and even less on economic thought, except perhaps as a historical curiosity. The philosophies underlying the moral presuppositions of mercantilism, with their related policies and instruments of enforcement, had tremendous influence on philosophers of the Scottish Enlightenment, particularly Adam Smith, his venerable teacher Francis Hutcheson, and his closest friend David Hume, all of whom would offer different systems of ethics and political economy.

## Economic Systems: Physiocracy (and Laissez-Faire)

Adam Smith maintained that physiocracy, "the agricultural systems of political œconomy," was a reaction to the established hegemony of mercantilism, more the product of a lively imagination than anything really substantive. It held that a country's prosperity derives from its agricultural wealth. Smith introduces his brief coverage rather dismissively:

47. Quoted in Edgar S. Furniss, *The Position of the Laborer in a System of Nationalism* (Boston: Houghton Mifflin, 1920), 114–15.

> That system which represents the produce of land as the sole source of the revenue and wealth of every country has, so far as I know, never been adopted by any nation, and it at present exists only in the speculations of a few men of great learning and ingenuity in France. It would not, surely, be worth while to examine at great length the errors of a system which never has done, and probably never will do any harm in any part of the world. I shall endeavour to explain, however, as distinctly as I can, the great outlines of this very ingenious system.[48]

It was this ingenuity that merited some brief accounting. Additionally, because of his heavy use of major elements of the physiocratic school in his "circular flow" analysis of the macroeconomy, it is tempting to think that Smith may have felt somewhat of a personal obligation, however slight, to make mention of a system authored by the creative geniuses of French physiocrats François Quesnay and Anne-Robert-Jacques Turgot, savants he had met in Paris a few years earlier at one of the literary salons he was prone to frequent, as mentioned earlier.

With land as the only source of wealth, the physiocrats held that of the three classes of society—the agricultural class, the artisan class, and the landowning class—it was only the agricultural class, labor, that was productive and responsible for the creation and distribution of wealth. The artisans, although unproductive, received salaries, while landowners, even though they held the source of agricultural product from which they derived rental payments, were themselves unproductive—a concept that Smith, of course, considered anathema.

The creation of economic wealth, so understood, would benefit immeasurably by little government involvement in the form of taxation. In fact, only the net product of land should be taxed, and

48. *WN*, 663–88; quotation on p. 663.

this system of commerce should be left free to pursue economic gains entirely unfettered by state oversight or regulation. This philosophy has been labeled "laissez-faire," an approach to economic policy that focuses on an absence of government policy in a nation's economic affairs. It is maintained by many that Quesnay originated the phrase, although it does not appear in his foundational physiocrat publication "General Maxims for the Economic Government of an Agricultural Kingdom."[49] Like the catchphrase "invisible hand," "laissez-faire" "(leave us alone" or "leave it to us") has been carelessly and inappropriately bandied about as representing the political philosophy undergirding the free-market system Adam Smith constructed in *WN*.

The history of this provocative phrase is much more intriguing and has nothing to do with Adam Smith.[50] Around 1681 (over forty decades before Smith's birth). the French finance minister and first minister of state under Louis XIV, Jean-Baptiste Colbert (1619–83), framer and relentless promoter of the mercantilist policies of a specific French variety ("Colbertism"), met with a group of businessmen inquiring what the state could do for them to help promote business. The context was an overregulated French market economy. He was met with this simple and brief response from a

49. Found at https://www.marxists.org/reference/subject/economics/quesnay/1767/maxims.htm.

50. The following three paragraphs draw on material from these sources: Gavin Kennedy, "Adam Smith: Some Popular Uses and Abuses," in Hanley, *Adam Smith: His Life*, 462; Ian Simpson Ross, *The Life of Adam Smith* (Oxford: Oxford University Press, 1995), xxvi, 274–75; Jerry Z. Muller, *Adam Smith in His Time and Ours* (Princeton, NJ: Princeton University Press, 1995), 25; Gavin Kennedy, *An Authentic Account of Adam Smith* (Cham, Switzerland: Palgrave Macmillan, 2017), 108–9, 155–58; "*Laissez-faire*," in Wikipedia, at https://en.wikipedia.org/wiki/Laissez-faire; D. H. MacGregor, *Economic Thought and Policy* (Oxford: Oxford University Press, 1949); John Maynard Keynes, *The End of Laissez-Faire* (London: Hogarth, 1926), at https://www.panarchy.org/keynes/laissezfaire.1926.html. The essay by Keynes, which was published as a pamphlet by the Hogarth Press in July 1926, was based on the Sidney Ball Lecture given by him at Oxford in November 1924 and on his June 1926 lecture at the University of Berlin.

"plain spoken" French merchant, M. le Gendre, the leader of the group: "laissez-nous-faire" ("let us do [it]" or "leave us alone"). Over half a century later, word of this exchange reached a French minister of foreign affairs, René-Louis de Voyer de Paulmy, marquis d'Argenson (1694–1757), who apparently noted it in his diary in 1736 ("let go, which should be the motto of all public power"). In 1751, he published an article in the *Journal économique* and this constitutes the first official appearance of "laisser faire" in recorded scholarly history. Adam Smith was roughly 27 years old and just installed as the University of Glasgow's professor of logic and rhetoric.

Quesnay's disciple, and, with him, leader of the physiocrat school, Vincent de Gournay (1712–59), was a strong proponent of the removal of trade restrictions and the deregulation of industry in France. Employing Quesnay's writings on China, he expanded the "laissez-faire" mantra to the fuller maxim "laissez-faire et laissez-passer" ("let do and let pass"). Subsequent history considers this act to represent official codification of the phrase.

In 1757, physiocrat Turgot used the term "laissez-faire" in an article prepared for the prestigious *Encyclopédie,* coedited by Jean le Rond d'Alembert (1717–83) , and he credited the phrase's origins to Gournay.

We conclude with Kennedy's assertion:

> Let us be clear: Adam Smith did not use the words "Laissez-faire" in anything that he wrote, published in his lifetime or posthumous, or in any student notes that have so far been found, or in any reports of his lectures by those who attended them (John Millar, James Woodrow, Lord Buchan, John Stuart, etc.,) or by those who knew him intimately (such as Dugald Stewart, whose father was a student at Glasgow with Smith)....
>
> We know that Smith knew of the use and meaning of laissez-faire from his close association with the Physiocratic circle around Quesnay during his visits to Paris (1764–67).

> The fact is that laissez-faire never entered his vocabulary. Nor did an English translation. This has not prevented many commentators from seeking to use Smith's use of Natural Liberty as a synonym for laissez-faire. It was not the same thing.[51]

Despite the deeply misguided philosophical and practical direction of the physiocratic school, it was here that political economy received its first exposure to quantitative method and analysis. Quesnay, as royal physician, applied his physiological observations of the flow and circulation of blood within the human body to economic science, created a rudimentary economic model, and published the entire work in 1758 as *Tableau économique*. But the quasi-mathematical content of *Tableau* and the associated papers offer us more than just an initial quantitative turn. It is a creative construction, however rudimentary, of a "circular flow" model, an attempt to illustrate the various flows of income and expenses among the three strata of the physiocrats' agricultural society. It is also an early economic balance sheet. Quesnay compiled a volume of all his significant work, which was published as *Physiocratie* (1767–68), and he gifted Adam Smith with a copy. Some of his propositions would find their way into the macroeconomic considerations in *WN*, if in more sophisticated form, as Smith applied these concepts to his political economy, but they were framed by a "simple system of natural liberty . . . [where] every man, as long as he does not violate the laws of justice, is left perfectly free to pursue his own interest his own way, and to bring both his industry and capital into competition with those of any other man or order of men." With such a system in place, "the sovereign has only three duties to attend to."[52]

51. Gavin Kennedy, "Adam Smith and the Myth of Laissez Faire," quoted at https://economistsview.typepad.com/economistsview/2012/06/adam-smith-and-the-myth-of-laissez-faire.html.

52. *WN*, 687; Ross, *Life*, 215–17, 278–79.

Despite Adam Smith's perpetual reminders that commercial society functions optimally without the involvement of the state, he does advise a crucial role for government in three broad areas—an irreducible minimum, as it were, for government involvement in society.

## The Place of the State: Responsibilities, Expenditures, and Revenues

Governmental defense spending ranks highest. According to Smith's stadial model of historical progression, cultures advance from the crudest state (hunting and pasturing) to the most developed (the exchange economy) with correspondingly greater need for defense. As population, capital stock, and technology grow, production expands and security concerns call forth more and better defense. The attendant complexities of a more integrated and interdependent society often cause internal distortions, unrest, and vulnerability to foreign invasion, which can require military mobilization.[53]

Ensuring justice between members of society is the second rationale for devoting government attention to matters of state. In this case, the role of civil authorities is to protect property owners. Drawing on similar principles proposed earlier in *TMS*, Smith maintains that human nature will set the rich and poor against each other, since the rich are ambitious and avaricious, while the poor disdain work and love "present ease and enjoyment"—two opposing propensities that are both predictable and universal. We notice here the growing concern for the security of private property, requiring the protection of the government. Because "the violation of justice is what men will never submit to from one another, the public magistrate is under a necessity

53. *WN*, 689–708.

of employing the power of the commonwealth to enforce the practice of this virtue."[54]

Having taken care of defense and justice, the third and final responsibility of the state is to provide public works and institutions for "facilitating the commerce of the society" and "promoting the instruction of the people." The former involves both government and private interests, depending on how incentivized private industry is to promote commerce. To be clear, Smith never proposes public projects as a substitute for private enterprise. In fact, he maintains that, where possible, publicly funded commercial endeavors should adhere to a "user pay" principle. Meanwhile, however, state support for certain aspects of foreign trade is justified since traders often require extra protection from, for example, "barbarous and uncivilized nations" or need to locate foreign ambassadors in other parts of the world.[55]

The final category for which public funds are required is education, in order to offset the mind-numbing effects of the division of labor and specialization. Publicly funded education is not an escape hatch for the lower classes, but a means to ensure a more prosperous, happy, and just society. Smith is channeling both Plato and Aristotle here and follows up with some recommendations for educational curricula. Postsecondary education, however, should not be supported by the state, since—using his personal experience at Oxford as one example—the large endowments at such institutions have already disincentivized instructors to excel in teaching. Publicly funded universities are as corrupt as merchant monopolies and trade guilds because their remuneration is not geared to performance. The objective of public education is social stability, while higher education should provide the quality education required to be successful

54. *WN*, 708–23, and *TMS*, 340.
55. *WN*, 723–58.

at a trade. Smith also recommends education as a remedy for those whose religious "fanaticism" has placed them in the grip of superstition and who may thus pose a threat to civic society. Finally, the "dignity" of the sovereign justifies the financial support of the public.[56]

Public expenditures are financed by tax revenue or borrowing, and Smith sets forth four principles as guideposts for a tax system: progressivity (higher income earners pay at a higher tax rate), clarity and predictability, convenience, and efficiency in collection. He weighs in on the fairness and unfairness of various types of tax, including associated nuances such as tax levies and tax incidence, and even issues related to tax evasion.[57]

If the state fails to recoup its public expenditures through taxation, it must take on debt, but only as a last resort, because debt redirects scarce resources to less than optimal allocations. Debt financing burdens future generations. Governments would be better off funding war as expenditures are incurred and do what they can to anticipate and finance expenditures—even war costs—out of current or future budgeted tax revenue.[58] Ending on a critical note regarding Britain's current indebtedness, Adam Smith concludes his political economy with a recommendation that the American colonies be set free, since the maintenance of colonial interests through debt financing is far too prohibitive and, as the historical financial records of other European empires show, those debts are rarely entirely repaid.[59]

We turn now to exploring the alignment of key themes in Adam Smith's political economy with those of the Christian thinker in the Reformed tradition.

56. *WN*, 758–816.
57. *WN*, 817–906.
58. *WN*, 925–26.
59. *WN*, 907–47.

## Christian Theistic Evaluation

The Scriptures teach morality, both propositionally and through relatable narratives that provide a meaningful source of moral guidance and ethics. This helps us navigate the complexity of moral reality and instructs us in normative ethical behavior. Thus, while Scripture is no textbook for political economy or economic science by standards of the twenty-first-century academy, it does prescribe particular behavioral precepts. We can assert, therefore, that from their social location in the redemptive pilgrimage to the city from the garden—the realized kingdom of God—people have plenty of guidance, with love for God and love for neighbor as the north star.

In the Reformed understanding, love for neighbor is a seamless way of demonstrating one's devotion to the Creator, and such neighborly concern is actualized by striving toward "human flourishing." Although this nomenclature is now found in almost all the theoretical and practical (non-Christian) literature on economic development, it carries a particular connotation in Christian theism or the Reformed tradition. Human flourishing is God's chief design for redeemed humans created in his image and for his glory. Because such flourishing encapsulates both the spiritual and the physical dimension, we are brought immediately into the world of economics—material well-being and health. And in light of humanity's image-bearing capacity, we are all moral agents. Just as there is no metaphysical neutrality, so there can be no morally neutral epistemology or ethic. Moral presuppositions and consequences attach to all our reality. Thoughts, speech, and activity are driven by principles of morality, whether consciously or subconsciously. There are moral absolutes. Specifically, even human reasoning and human use of logic are dependent on knowledge of God and are guided by it, because human beings, in their very character as the image of God, as Cornelius Van Til often puts it, should "think God's thoughts after him." Human knowledge, therefore, is "analogical," being ultimately dependent on divine knowledge. Sin weakens the human capacity for moral thinking and behavior (the noetic effects of sin), but it does not destroy the human constitution as rational and moral, and so we remain responsible for our behavior. All facts and events have meaning given by their author, the self-contained ontological Trinity.[60]

I go to some lengths to remind us of this because until the middle of the twentieth century, political economy was understood to be a primarily normative endeavor, concerned with things as they should be—a decidedly ethical stance. Although always evolving to some degree, as disciplines do, economics as a science had its origins with the late nineteenth-century marginalist revolution sparked by William Stanley Jevons (1835–82) and others. With the incorporation of mathematics and quantitative procedures, along with "utility thinking," into the realm of political economy, and following the introduction of the thought of Milton Friedman (1912–2006) at the University of Chicago, the neoclassical turn was complete, with its emphasis on economic method now articulated as solving the problem of constrained maximization: utility for the individual and profitability for the firm, the two players on the field of microeconomics, subject to the constraints imposed by budgets.[61] Or, to put it starkly, the early classical school, for the most part, saw people in society as social beings; the neoclassical school

60. See, for example, the discussion of Cornelius Van Til in *Christian Theistic Ethics* (Phillipsburg, NJ: Presbyterian and Reformed, 1980), 18–40.

61. The distinction between value and fact in philosophy provides the methodological basis for distinctions between what is positive and what is normative. David Hume defined a "matter of fact" as something that could be directly perceived with one of the five senses. Current positivist science, however, now poses facts that cannot be verified in this manner. In *A System of Logic*, John Stuart Mill employed Hume's fact-value distinction in defining the science and art of economics. See Jan Peil and Irene van Staveren, *Handbook of Economics and Ethics* (Cheltenham, UK: Edward Elgar, 2009).

considered each person as an autonomous individual seeking personal utility maximization—a calculating, utilitarian, individual consumer, whose motivations and actions are defined in psychological terms. With the imprimatur of Irving Fisher (1867–1947), arguably the first economist to be considered wholly neoclassical, the corner was irrevocably turned.

This view of humanity—*homo economicus* it has come to be called—has deep roots, however, dating all the way back to John Stuart Mill (1806–73), a political economist with strong utilitarian leanings, who famously claimed that political economy "does not treat the whole of man's nature as modified by the social state, nor of the whole conduct of man in society. It is concerned with him solely as a being who desires to possess wealth, and who is capable of judging the comparative efficacy of means for obtaining that end."[62] Pure rationality and perfect knowledge and information become the order of the (epistemological) day. In fact, however, some variant of this idea goes back to Xenophon and Plato.[63]

Keeping in mind the foundational Reformed Christian principles identified in chapter 3 and the foregoing brief summary of economic history, we now test the claim that Adam Smith's political economy reaches the moral stature required by the Reformed Christian tradition. Our typology traced out above obliges the topical coverages that ultimately have to do, in the first instance, with the key teachings of human flourishing. We will map these central distinctives over the "greatest working-man's tract ever

62. John Stuart Mill, "On the Definition of Political Economy, and on the Method of Investigation Proper to It," *London and Westminster Review*, October 1836; Mill, *Essays on Some Unsettled Questions of Political Economy*, 2nd ed. (London: Longmans, Green, Reader & Dyer, 1874), essay 5, paragraphs 38 and 48.

63. David Wilson and William Dixon, *A History of Homo Economicus: The Nature of the Moral in Economic Theory* (London: Routledge, 2014). These authors illustrate the evolving and multifaceted meaning of the concept *homo economicus* over the history of the term.

written"[64] and close with some summary observations.

## Thematic Analysis

### Stewardship and Labor

The command to love one's neighbor as oneself and the Reformed understanding of the cultural mandate result in a fourfold restorative injunction for citizens inhabiting both the already and the not yet. This process of multidimensional renewal has stewardship as the driving principle, a concept which the Merriam-Webster dictionary defines as "the activity or job of protecting and being responsible for something" or "the careful and responsible management of something entrusted to one's care."[65] A business executive, in his reflections on the responsibilities of information technology, puts it like this: "Stewardship is defined as an ethic that embodies the responsible planning and management of resources." This includes both efficiency and effectiveness. The former he defines as the "ability to avoid wasting materials, energy, efforts, money, and time in doing or in producing a desired result," while the latter is defined as achieving the desired outcome.[66] It turns out that this decidedly contemporary sense of stewardship has much in common with that of the self-consciously Reformed Christian. Hear R. C. Sproul:

64. K. Haakonssen, "Smith, Adam (1763–90)," in *The Routledge Encyclopedia of Philosophy*," ed. E. Craig (London: Routledge, 1998), quoted in Griswold, *Virtues of Enlightenment*, 261.

65. https://www.merriam-webster.com/dictionary/stewardship#:~:text=%3A%20the%20conducting%2C%20supervising%2C%20or,stewardship%20of%20natural%20resources.

66. Henry C. Scoles, "Stewardship, Efficiency and Effectiveness," July 3, 2018, at https://www.linkedin.com/pulse/stewardship-efficiency-effectiveness-henry-scoles/. Technology's impact on human dignity and the human spirit has not, however, been unambiguously good.

> On the very first page of the Bible, we see the creation of human beings—made in the image of God, who revealed Himself initially as the Creator of all things—and the subsequent call of His image bearers to imitate Him in a certain way: by being productive. Human beings were commanded to be fruitful and multiply. This was a command for productivity, which has stewardship implications. Thus, the concern for stewardship is rooted in creation.[67]

Abraham Kuyper (1837–1920) regularly and passionately addressed the tremendous social and economic injustices of the decades around the turn of the twentieth century, always with an eye to the revolutionary era that consumed the waning years of Adam Smith's life. The combined spirit of both the French and the Industrial Revolutions had spawned secularism and wealth-seeking individualism, which he saw as the formative consciousness of the modern period. The resulting spiritual and social anomie, and the widening gap between the rich and the poor, he designated the "social problem," and he challenged his audience and society as a whole to return to the principle of love for neighbor and responsible use of material resources:

> All our possessions are only held on loan from [God]. We manage our possessions only as a form of stewardship. . . . O, it is so profoundly untrue that the Word of God only calls us to save our souls. No, God's Word poses firm ordinances and draws unmistakable lines also for our life as a nation and for our common social life.[68]

67. R. C. Sproul, "What Is Biblical Stewardship?" (2016), at https://www.ligonier.org/learn/articles/what-biblical-stewardship.

68. Abraham Kuyper, "The Social Question and the Christian Religion," trans. Harry Van Dyke, in *On Business and Economics*, ed. Peter S. Heslam (Bellingham, WA: Lexham, 2015), 217–19. This is Kuyper's historic opening address at the

Stewardship is indeed a creation ordinance, evidencing one's life commitment to principles of proper motive, self-control (Adam Smith's concept of "self-command"), and self-sacrifice.[69]

The Scriptures in their entirety, but particularly in the New Testament, further flesh out this concept of stewardship. Faithful stewardship extends to labor, industry, and productivity, all principles found in the teaching on work and thrift and in the narratives and parables of Jesus. There is an undeniable emphasis on fruitfulness for the sake of the kingdom. Productive human labor is a creation ordinance.[70]

Finally, the confessional documents associated with the Reformed tradition, most commonly called "subordinate standards," have a wealth of teaching on these matters. A veritable embarrassment of riches is found particularly in the commentaries on the decalogue in both the Heidelberg Catechism and the Westminster Standards. In addition to employing the Socratic method of pedagogy, the instructive practice in which the explanation of each proscriptive law is balanced by an equally important mandate to heed the implied prescription (and vice versa), and the deeper implications of each, constitute a treasure trove of wisdom for the conduct of men and women in society. Stewardship, labor, productivity, responsible and efficient use of resources, circumspect lifestyles and frugality,[71] thrift, and concern for the less fortunate are all elements of the Christian

Christian Social Congress, Amsterdam, November 9–12, 1891. It has undergone multiple translations.

69. "The Defining Characteristics of a Good and Faithful Steward," *Biblical Stewardship*, Feb. 23, 2018, at https://www.taylor.edu/news/the-defining-characteristics-of-a-good-and-faithful-steward#:~:text=The%20good%20and%20faithful%20steward,of%20how%20subtle%20or%20how.

70. Sproul, "Biblical Stewardship"; John Murray, *Principles of Conduct: Aspects of Biblical Ethics* (Grand Rapids: Eerdmans, 1957), 35–39, 82–106.

71. "Frugality," said Abraham Kuyper, "is still practiced in good Reformed families" ("Meditations," trans. Harry Van Dyke, in *Business and Economics*, 373).

theist or Reformed understanding of humanity's place in society before God, self, neighbor, and the created order.

Adam Smith's "working man's tract" opens with a ringing endorsement of precisely this creation ordinance: labor and productivity. Productivity is maximized through the division of labor; the economic and social conditions and structures in commercial society must be developed in such a way as to ensure maximum physical output. This furthers overall economic development and the wealth of nations, and it brings people out of their economically undeveloped state. Talents and skills must be recognized and applied to the tasks where they are most fully optimized. There is no room for wasted capabilities and expertise or for "unproductive labor" that does not add to material well-being, but is rather a cost to society because it is paid out of revenue, rather than capital, and tends to laziness. This group lives off the fruit of productive members of society, which violates a central principle—industriousness—necessary to an orderly and responsible commercial society.[72] The results of this reality are multidimensional. Firstly, resources expended on unproductive labor are resources not available for capital deepening (and widening). This interrupts the dynamic of wealth creation by redirecting a resource (money provided to the unproductive sector in commercial society) away from factors that ensure continuing improvements in a nation's wealth, as we have seen in Smith's theory of distribution and exchange. Secondly, this short-circuits the efficiencies gained through the allocative mechanism, by leaving fewer resources for saving. The tautological relationship between investment in productive capital stock and saving means less expenditure on productive capacity. Commercial society can invest in productive capital stock only to the degree that it saves. Finally, and related to this, is the principle of thrift

72. *WN*, 332–36. I am focusing here on the general concepts of "productive" and "unproductive" labor, not the outmoded and peculiar categories Smith uses.

and frugality. Smith considered frugality to be a predominating principle in human nature—even mentioning taxation as a possible way to curb prodigality. Saving is prompted by the desire for improvement in the material realm and "comes with us from the womb."[73] Frugality and thrift are hallmarks of Adam Smith's system.

In the same way, Smith's unmitigated passion for the protection of the working class and the weak in society is noteworthy.[74] Already early in *WN*, Smith categorically affirms that absent of anti-collusion legislation, employers "always and everywhere" collude to suppress wages since workers are forbidden by law to unite. This early indication of where Smith's sympathies lie in owner-labor relations gathers steam through his work, particularly as he touches on monopolies, poverty, and economic development. The unfettered, free economic exchange that characterizes competitive markets is the key to growth and the subsequent spread of wealth, a benefit that is particularly noticed among the lower echelon, the majority of a political society. It must, then, undoubtedly be the case that "no society can surely be flourishing and happy, of which the far greater part of the members are poor and miserable."[75] Similar sentiment was expressed over a century later during the economic depression of the 1880s in the Netherlands that uncovered the darker side of industrialization. Abraham Kuyper was driven to formulate a political philosophy on the run, as it were, in defusing class struggle on the brink of becoming class warfare. In one of a series of newspaper columns in February 1889, he intoned: "History clearly teaches that a confrontation cannot be avoided if the majority of the population lives

73. *WN*, 341.

74. On precisely this issue, see the parallel concern demonstrated by Abraham Kuyper in his entire oeuvre, but particularly in *Our Program: A Christian Political Manifesto*, trans. and ed. Harry Van Dyke (Bellingham, WA: Lexham, 2015), in the chapter entitled "The Social Question," 331–50. According to Kuyper, the entire system of jurisprudence in the late nineteenth- and early twentieth-century Netherlands was biased in favor of the rich and powerful.

75. *WN*, 96.

for many years with anxiety and resentment and so grows weaker in its moral fiber."[76] Societal happiness can be brought about through the intentional generosity and concern of the employer, since happy and healthy workers are more productive.[77] Adam Smith will always vindicate the "common man," the working class. Along similar lines, he expresses poorly disguised scorn for landowners who "earn" their rent, a "monopoly price," through no effort of their own, but whose "indolence" is the "natural effect of the ease and security of their situation."[78] Rent costs are, ultimately, determined by the amount of the land the tenant puts in use, itself a function of the population.[79] But because land always produces more than required, and while this surplus returns even higher returns to the landlord, the rental cost to the farmer is offset by the overall benefit to society at large.[80]

Adam Smith's demonstrated concern for the poor and those victimized by the commercial system is highly commendable and resonates well with the Christian theist. His focus on efficiency in production, through the specialization of labor, and the tremendous benefits that gains for the rising general economic welfare of commercial society, folds in well with the responsibility of all people to seek the flourishing of all humanity in material and spiritual well-being. But only in part.

## Education

Does the human flourishing flowing from Adam Smith's prescription of resource use and the human and material efficiencies resulting from the division of labor necessarily entail flourishing in

76. Kuyper, "Manual Labor," ed. Harry Van Dyke, trans. Reinder Bruinsma, in *Business and Economics*, 145.

77. *WN*, 82–104.

78. *WN*, 161, 265.

79. Although Smith does discuss improvements to land (and the corresponding increase in rents), his comments largely pertain to the nobility of Scotland who owned large tracts of land.

80. *WN*, 160–264.

the spiritual realm? Plainly put, is there a downside to people doing the same thing over and over again in assembly-line fashion? The answer is yes, absolutely; in fact, Smith's focus on good stewardship, as it benefits society in a material way, comes at a high price. He is the first to recognize the human cost, and his concern for the dignity and development of humanity motivates him to come up with a solution: education.

We should not diminish the value of this recommendation for a working-class laborer to whose defense Smith instinctively and regularly comes, in a society dominated by what we would today call classicism—the entrenched opposition between the owners and the workers. In that light, then, this is how Smith describes the repetitive, mind-numbing effects of labor specialization:

> The man whose whole life is spent in performing a few [repetitive] simple operations . . . generally becomes as stupid and ignorant as it is possible for a human creature to become. The torpor of his mind renders him, not only incapable of relishing or bearing a part of any rational conversation, but of conceiving any generous, noble, or tender sentiment.[81]

Because it is by far the greater part of society that lives by its labor, it is an exigency arising from labor specialization that must necessarily be addressed. An unthinking automaton represents a risk to the stability of society, even to the nation. Such a person is incapable of taking care of himself and unable to defend his country in wartime because he does not understand the issues or the life of a soldier. All the laborer knows is the employment "to which he has been bred," which has cost him his "intellectual, social, and martial virtues."[82] Virtuous commercial society cannot be constructed

81. *WN*, 782.
82. *WN*, 782.

successfully when this is the state of the "far greater part . . . of the great body of the people." Good government and an orderly society are features of a happy and peaceful social order, particularly in commercial society. It is incumbent upon government, therefore, to act in order "to prevent the almost entire corruption and degeneracy of the great body of the people."[83]

## Government

Adam Smith's analytical presentation of the static and dynamic features of the macroeconomy is regularly framed in moral terms, not least regarding the use of precious resources on what he considers frivolous expenditures. This explains why his indictment of government officials is particularly vehement, cast in terms of private versus public waste. "Great nations," he says, "are never impoverished by private, though they sometimes are by publick prodigality and misconduct. The whole, or almost the whole publick revenue, is in most countries employed in maintaining unproductive hands." Among such unproductive endeavor we must include the trappings of high society, the "ecclesiastical establishment," and the military in both peacetime and war. Such people produce nothing, being "maintained by the produce of other men's labor."[84] Potentially the numbers could get so large that the cost of supporting these parasitic profligates would outweigh the national output available for their support, although experience has shown that productive labor's income has been able to support both this group's private prodigality and also the "publick extravagance of government."[85]

Yet despite its lack of productive enterprise, there is still a place for government—minimal to be sure, but necessary for the flourishing of community in commercial society. Adam Smith's system

83. *WN*, 781.
84. *WN*, 342.
85. *WN*, 342–43.

of natural liberty conjoined with free market economics facilitates a political philosophy marked by minimal state oversight. After all, in a society marked by the virtues of beneficence and justice, Smith's prescription for government—its character and function—holds much in common with that in Scripture and reinforced in the teachings of the Reformed Christian tradition, particularly, again, in the confessional standards. Divinely appointed government acts as the central regulator of society, exercising its derived authority to establish order in its pursuit of earthly justice and protection. While recognizing that ultimate justice is within God's jurisdiction alone, God's agent of justice on earth must seek the good of all its subjects. "The highest and most sacred attribute of the sovereign," asserts Abraham Kuyper, "is that he upholds justice," which God himself then sustains through people's conscience, through punishment both in the present and at the last judgment, and through human intermediaries.[86] Article 13 of the *Manifesto* reads:

> [It is the responsibility of the sovereign] that by means of an independent judiciary, accessible to all and in keeping with the moral sense of justice in the nation and in accordance with laws founded on the eternal principles of justice, first, that it decide all disputes between parties, both of civil and administrative law; second, that it pronounce sentence against anyone who offends against the public order; and third, that it execute punishment on the convicted, not just to protect society or to improve the offender, but in the first place to restore violated justice, if need be by the death penalty which government in principle has the right to impose.[87]

86. Kuyper, *Our Program*, 211.

87. Kuyper, *Our Program*, 211. See also his *On Charity and Justice*, ed. Matthew J. Tuininga (Bellingham, WA: Lexham, 2022).

Society crumbles without the rule of law. For Adam Smith, too, justice is the main pillar upon which social life is built and is, in that regard, different from other virtues.[88]

But for all his emphasis on justice in both *TMS* and *WN*, as the socially and politically indispensable virtue binding together all of society, the concept is nowhere defined. Moreover, while Samuel Fleischacker offers a useful reconstruction of Smith's theory of justice, he is forced to conclude that Smith's concept of justice plays but a background role in *WN*, is usually almost inextricably tied to issues of utility, relies on a conventional notion of justice, and for these reasons does not constitute a unique or original contribution to this subject, as he had wished.[89] And while judging Smith's theory to be "highly original," Nicholas Wolterstorff agrees with Fleischacker that Smith lacks a theory of justice, and says that what he does present is actually more a theory of "injustice." By focusing on what Wolterstorff labels the "life-goods" and "life-evils" of a person (what Fleischacker has identified as the "utilitarian" concern), Wolterstorff rightly concludes that Smith neglects entirely the idea of human value and dignity in his account of injustice, even though his concern for human dignity "most definitely" plays a role in his thought generally; it is particularly evident in his social theory.[90] The Christian theist will find in Nicholas Wolterstorff and in Abraham Kuyper holistic accounts of jurisprudence in general and justice in particular.

88. *TMS*, 86; David Lieberman, "Adam Smith on Justice, Rights, and Law," in *The Cambridge Companion to Adam Smith*, ed. Knud Haakonssen (Cambridge: Cambridge University Press, 2006), 214–45.

89. Fleischacker, *Philosophical Companion*, 166–73.

90. Nicholas Wolterstorff, "Adam Smith on Justice and Injustice," in Hanley, *Adam Smith: His Life*, 173–91. See also Wolterstorff, *Justice: Rights and Wrongs* (Princeton, NJ: Princeton University Press: 2008). He argues that no secular account of natural human rights is successful and provides a theistic account of justice by combining moral philosophy and Christian ethics to develop an important theory of rights and of justice as grounded in rights.

For Smith, key among government's duties of jurisprudence is the upholding of remedial and commutative justice. While he says next to nothing about distributive justice, his uneasiness about the appropriation of economic power by large commercial interests, such as monopolies, shows his sensitivity to the potential for abuse by big business. He was clearly worried about the potential for the overreach of free market economic structures. Economic injustice is of great concern to him, whether it is driven by greed, or due to government regulation, or the result of market failure. This is confirmed by his opposition to tariffs and any other interference in the free flow of goods domestically and abroad, which is one reason for his strong stance against mercantilism and unbridled free market economic activity (what is called "laissez-faire" today). Any situation that threatens an individual's natural liberty and places him in social or economic subservience demands redress and requires government action to avoid or remedy it.

The avoidance of economic and often related social inequities is best maintained by the rule of law to ensure the protection of property and associated rights and to honor integrity in contracts. This is vital to a well-functioning commercial society. As the Westminster Larger Catechism puts it in Q&A 141, "The duties required in the eighth commandment are, truth, faithfulness, and justice in contracts and commerce between man and man; rendering to every one his due; restitution of goods unlawfully detained from the right owners thereof; giving and lending freely, according to our abilities, and the necessities of others . . . and an endeavour, by all just and lawful means, to procure, preserve, and further the wealth and outward estate of others, as well as our own." And in Q&A 142, there follows a long list of "sins forbidden," all in the economic realm.[91] This was the society that Smith was seeking to construct.

91. *The Confession of Faith, the Larger and Shorter Catechisms, with the Scripture Proofs at Large* (Glasgow: Free Presbyterian Publications, 1994), 225–27.

From Adam Smith's views on government responsibility for defense (foreign and domestic) and public services, to his recommendations on expenditure and taxation, there is good reason why his council for minimal government strikes a familiar chord with the Reformed Christian. The ethical center of the commercial society Smith prescribes bears much resemblance to the catechisms he memorized at his mother's knee.

## Economic Development, Human Flourishing, and Poverty

As much as Adam Smith contributed to mainstream economic thought in analyzing the socioeconomic world of rich economies, he was, as Amartya Sen points out, "in fact, a major development economist," who pioneered an interdisciplinary approach to the process of economic development.[92] Speaking even more broadly, Max Hartwell avers that "economics is, in essence, the study of poverty."[93] In agreement, Ryan Patrick Hanley observes: "The fundamental departure point for Smith's defense of commercial society is its capacity to provide for the poor."[94]

We disrespect Adam Smith if we neglect *WN* as constituting a major treatise on economic development, and it must be regarded as such by scholars and policymakers who are serious about improving the human condition. Smith maintains that commercial society fosters moral conduct and thus promotes virtue, such as human well-being.[95] What was earlier observed in *TMS* we

92. Amartya Sen, "Adam Smith and Economic Development," in Hanley, *Adam Smith: His Life*, 281, 286. The need for such an interdisciplinary approach is now recognized by development economists.

93. Quoted by Martin Ravallion on the homepage of the website accompanying his book *The Economics of Poverty: History, Measurement, and Policy* (New York: Oxford University Press, 2016), at https://economicsandpoverty.com/.

94. Ryan Patrick Hanley, *Adam Smith and the Character of Virtue* (New York: Cambridge University Press, 2009), 18.

95. On the very first page of his massive treatise, the fourth paragraph, Smith maintains that poverty is a root cause of infanticide and the fatal abandonment of

now see reinforced in *WN*: Adam Smith was committed to happiness, understood as human flourishing.[96] Although this *summum bonum* differs from that of the Christian theist, for whom the chief good is the kingdom of God, Smith's emphasis is missed by most Smithian scholars, who fail to perceive this more holistic teaching.

Ryan Patrick Hanley has observed this lacuna in Smith studies as well, and he notes that Smith eschewed both the extreme of boundless optimism and the extreme of "hard-nosed" pessimism: "Adam Smith . . . seems to have discovered a very different sort of solace—an optimism that is guarded, perhaps, yet genuine. In so doing, he gives us reasons for hope, too."[97]

## Human Flourishing: The Kuyperian Tradition

The Reformed tradition represents a rich and varied source of encouragement and possibility in addressing the alleviation of poverty. Abraham Kuyper's insights, although dated, are helpful and even necessary in grounding the thinking of the Christian theist in the issues at stake in the amelioration of poverty and the advancement of human flourishing and culture. Kuyper's disciple, Bob Goudzwaard, has taken Kuyper's concern to heart and, like Kuyper, has dedicated his life to the pursuit of God-honoring and God-glorifying behavior in the realm of contemporary economics in the academy, business, government, and the public square, all in pursuit of human flourishing.[98] His concern is contemporary

---

the young, the elderly, and the sick (*WN*, 4). This very theme—the reduction to barbarity of the poverty-stricken—is, in fact, introduced earlier in *TMS*, 209–10.

96. Hanley, *Character of Virtue*, 13.

97. Hanley, *Character of Virtue*, 13–14. Hanley quotes "another subtle philosopher," P. G. Wodehouse, who opined, "Material comforts are all very well, but if the *summum bonum* is to be achieved, the Soul also demands a look in," in *The Clicking of Cuthbert* (1922; repr., Woodstock: Overlook Press, 2002), 3.

98. See, for example: Bob Goudzwaard, *Globalization and the Kingdom of God* (Grand Rapids: Baker Books, 2001); Bob Goudzwaard and Harry de Lange, *Beyond Poverty and Affluence: Toward an Economy of Care with a Twelve-Step Program for Economic Recovery* (Grand Rapids: Eerdmans, 1995); Goudzwaard, *Idols of Our*

society's worship at the altar of materialism and consumerism, addiction to GDP growth at all costs, infinite appetite for more of everything material, and flagrant disregard for the poor. He locates the root cause for this ontological reality of the human condition with the secularism and humanism of the French Revolution and the independent spirit fostered by the Enlightenment, in concert with the lasting technological and dehumanizing effects of the Industrial Revolution—which, recall, was born in the waning years of the life of Adam Smith.[99] With respect to alleviating poverty, in

---

*Time* (Downers Grove, IL: InterVarsity Press, 1984); Goudzwaard, *Aid for the Overdeveloped West* (Toronto, ON: Wedge Publishing, 1975). The earlier works are translations from the Dutch.

99. Despite the commonality between the Kuyperian/neo-Kuyperian tradition and Adam Smith, particularly when it comes to concern for poverty alleviation and human flourishing, that tradition is generally not friendly to Smith. I am thinking particularly of the Kuyper-Dooyeweerd-Goudzwaard axis and the mistaken attribution to Adam Smith of four concepts and their meaning: *homo economicus*, capitalism, laisser-faire, and the invisible hand. This animosity originated with Kuyper himself, was perpetuated by Herman Dooyeweerd (1894–1977, originator of the Reformational philosophy of neo-Calvinism), and was brought to fruition, in the field of political economy or economic science, by Goudzwaard (b. 1934). The central issue is really the lack of nuancing by these otherwise excellent scholars with respect to what Adam Smith himself believed and maintained in his work, and what his intellectual successors made of his work as they built upon the foundation he constructed.

To Smith has been attributed dehumanizing, mechanistic, and other characteristics found in the further development of economic thought in the marginalist, neoclassical, and mathematical schools. Firstly, Smith's views on human reason, among his other convictions (particularly made explicit in *TMS*), would disqualify any characterization of humans as solely rationalistic economic agents (*homo economicus*—the label first attached to Smith's successor, John Stuart Mill, by Mill's detractors). Further, recall that Smith never used the categories and labels "capitalism" and "laissez-faire." Recall our discussion above on some of these items. This portrayal of Smith is disingenuous and is comparable, for example, to attributing to John Calvin the neo-orthodoxy of Karl Barth and Emil Brunner.

For Kuyper's views, see particularly "Forewords" in *Business and Economics*, vii–xvii. The best foreword is Brian Fikkert's, as he correctly attributes to neoclassical economics the commitment of the concept of *homo economicus* (vii–xii). Paul Oslington's identification of Adam Smith as Kuyper's "fellow Calvinist" and his claim that Smith, like Kuyper, held to the doctrine of sin (as understood by the Reformed Christian orthodox) are quite a stretch (xiii)—although, as I mention in chapter 2 above, there

Smith-like fashion, Goudzwaard advocates justice for both the rich and the poor and the employment of wealth in the service of the poor (with the Church Fathers, particularly Chrysostom, he designates the property of the rich as a "social mortgage"). Christians' responsibility lies in contributing to a better world of dynamic justice and faithful stewardship. While "globalization is the highest expression of modernization" in Western culture, with its associated dependence on human rationality and on lack of dignity and stewardship, Goudzwaard sees hope in a current trend (in 2001) among international organizations and multinationals to accept their own "inalienable social responsibility" for human flourishing and put aside the idolatry of "self-chosen growth at all cost." Hope is found in our "willingness to hear the cries of

---

certainly seem to be sprinklings of Calvinism in what Smith holds. Finally, Kenneth Barnes correctly, but uncritically, presents Kuyper's unnuanced conviction that laissez-faire and capitalism are Smithian inventions (xv). Kuyper says precisely this in "The Social Question and the Christian Religion," 197n44. Finally, Kuyper has Smith dead wrong in attributing to him the complete abolition of tariffs—i.e., free trade without limits ("The Sacred Order," trans. Harry Van Dyke, in *Business and Economics*, 316). As we have noted above, there was always room for tariffs in Smith's thinking.

Herman Dooyeweerd's philosophical program is found in his *A New Critique of Theoretical Thought* (Philadelphia: Presbyterian and Reformed, 1953–58), translated from *De Wijsbegeerte der Wetsidee*, 3 vols. (Amsterdam: H. J. Paris, 1935–36). *New Critique* is a ponderous read. It essentially places responsibility for all the evils of the economic system of the day (capitalism) on the classical school of economics and its appropriation of Enlightenment thought, particularly faith in reason, science and *mathesis universalis*, progress, and the exaltation of the individual. This individualism, in economic terms, resulted in the rationalization of commercial life, with its "unrestrained free play of the social forces in economic life" seen in the mantra "laissez-faire, laissez-aller," the adage "propagated" by the classical school (*New Critique*, 2:337–65). Dooyeweerd's teaching on "The Humanistic Idea of mathesis universalis in pure economics" constitutes "possibly the most challenging page in his entire book," according to Samuel T. Wolfe, *A Key to Dooyeweerd* (Nutley, NJ: Presbyterian and Reformed, 1977) 79.

Bob Goudzwaard's corpus, specifically in the realm of economics and social philosophy, follows Dooyeweerd's critique of the classical school, but singles out the perceived misdeeds of Adam Smith in particular. See notably Part One in his otherwise excellent *Capitalism and Progress: A Diagnosis of Western Society* (Toronto, ON: Wedge Publishing, 1979).

the poor" and in our recognition that Jesus Christ is not only the Alpha and the Omega, but also the *arché* and *telos*—the source and fulfillment—of all aspects of life, including the family, economics, technology, and politics. Christ stands on the personal, political, economic, and social horizons. The world order that Goudzwaard identifies is a "stronger" globalization than the current materialistic one: the kingdom of Jesus Christ. "The reign of this coming Shepherd-King implies not the survival of the fittest but the rescue of the weakest. It is this stronger globalization which once will conquer the world, and in which light we already have to live now and here." Goudzwaard closes with the powerful advice of Dietrich Bonhoeffer in his *Ethics* that we are living in the "before-last" (*das Verletzte*): we should be living from the meaning that is coming from the end, and not only that of the beginning.[100] This is what it means to live *coram deo*, to inhabit the already/not yet.

This emphasis on hope, in concert with the emphasis on happiness in Adam Smith's concept of human flourishing, is being developed in certain centers of research,[101] and we will close this section optimistically on a note of hope.[102]

## Human Flourishing: The Multidisciplinary Imperative

The reservoir of the poor is inexhaustible, and so is concern for their plight. It appears that in a world dominated by fractious

100. Adrian Vlot and Bob Goudzwaard, "We Are People of the Way: An Impression of the Final Session of the Conference," *Philosophia Reformata* 66 (2001): 142–52.

101. For example, the Erasmus Happiness Economics Research Organisation (EHERO) is a scientific institute where happiness is studied. They define happiness as "the subjective enjoyment of one's life as a whole" (https://www.eur.nl/en/ehero/about-ehero).

102. The remainder of this section borrows from my "An Ontology of Human Flourishing: Economic Development and Epistemologies of Faith, Hope, and Love," in *Historical and Multidisciplinary Perspectives on Hope*, ed. Steven C. van den Heuvel (Cham, Switzerland: Springer, 2020), available at https://link.springer.com/chapter/10.1007/978-3-030-46489-9_13.

public discourse in every arena—political, intellectual, social, religious, and economic—concern for the poor seems to be innate to the human spirit. But while poverty alleviation is ostensibly the one totalizing metanarrative of a fragmented humanity, there is vast disagreement on poverty interventionist methodologies, policies, and practices. We all have a common goal; we need to agree on agencies and pathways to achieve it.

Such unanimous agreement on the problem opens the way for interdisciplinary research and dialogue in search of poverty alleviation solutions. The violence of poverty affects all areas of human health, and to fail in one vector of human flourishing is to fail in all. Economic deprivation, whether measured by relative or absolute standards of economic well-being, leads to a host of associated pathologies—breakdown in other facets of the human condition. In recognition of this, the United Nations has developed a metric that reflects concern for people and their capabilities in their assessment of a country's development status. This more holistic measure, the Human Development Index (HDI), goes beyond just economic factors and includes measures of health and education. It is noteworthy that this measure reflects the now common view that poverty is multidimensional.[103]

But poverty is much broader than even this, in categories largely unmeasurable, such as basic civil rights, social inclusion, and self-respect.[104] Any disambiguation of poverty must include the lived reality of social poverty often experienced by minority cultures, the emotional poverty associated with psychological and mental breakdown, and the spiritual poverty stemming from

103. See http://hdr.undp.org/en/content/human-development-index-hdi.

104. See the incisive, illuminating, and groundbreaking work in this area by 1998 economics Nobel laureate Amartya Sen in much of his work, notably *Development as Freedom* (Oxford: Oxford University Press, 1999). See also his *The Idea of Justice* (Cambridge, MA: Harvard University Press, 2009) and *On Economic Inequality* (Oxford: Oxford University Press, 1973).

people without that meaning in life often given by metaphysical constructs such as religion. The common end of all human florescence is personal happiness, dignity, self-worth, and participation in the divine, all of which provide gratification in body and spirit.[105]

It has been demonstrated that field experimentation in the field of development economics, utilizing the quantitative tools of microeconomics in implementing randomized control trials, has provided helpful but not exhaustive solutions to poverty alleviation.[106] Such research has shown that optimism and a hopeful spirit often lead to success, while a pessimistic spirit, fear of failure, and lack of self-confidence often result in failure.[107] This research has further delivered much more promising results than the historic solution to poverty alleviation offered by the top-down approach of Jeffrey D. Sachs,[108] which focuses on large-scale—typically governmental—aid to impoverished countries, or the more realistic bottom-up approach advocated by William R. Easterly, who is concerned to recognize and advance the dignity of the poor by bringing them into the solution themselves.[109]

While these foregoing multidisciplinary insights into improving the lot of humanity created in the image of God are luminous in their own right, and while the Reformed tradition esteems the common

105. van Vliet, "Ontology of Human Flourishing," 239–45.

106. See the work of 2019 economics Nobel laureates Abhijit V. Banerjee and Esther Duflo in many works, but particularly in their groundbreaking book *Poor Economics: A Radical Rethinking of the Way to Fight Global Poverty* (New York: Public Affairs, 2012).

107. van Vliet, "Ontology of Human Flourishing," 243–45.

108. See particularly his *The End of Poverty: Economic Possibilities for Our Time* (New York: Penguin, 2005) and his *Common Wealth: Economics for a Crowded Planet* (New York: Penguin, 2008).

109. Easterly does this in various ways. See his *The Elusive Quest for Growth: Economists' Adventures and Misadventures in the Tropics* (Cambridge, MA: MIT Press, 2001), *The White Man's Burden: Why the West's Efforts to Aid the Rest Have Done So Much Ill and So Little Good* (New York: Penguin, 2006), and *The Tyranny of Experts: Economists, Dictators, and the Forgotten Rights of the Poor* (New York: Basic Books, 2014).

grace inherent in a nonbelieving world, by which the Christian may lay claim to the wisdom of nonbelievers, we must stop short of any focus on human anthropology that ignores the biblical teaching on human flourishing. We must turn to theological anthropology and focus on those biblical categories that underlie the reality of the human condition. These categories flow from the theological virtues of faith, hope, and love.[110]

### Human Flourishing: Love, Faith, and Hope

The Christian-theistic metaphysic provides a powerful philosophical resource, even social philosophy, in addressing humanity's general concern for the poor. We ask, What are the relative roles of faith, hope, and love?

Note that, firstly, the chief of these virtues is love, a divinely infused habit which inclines the human will to cherish God, above all else, for his own sake. And then we esteem fellow humanity for the sake of God. The reciprocity associated with Christians' love of God, in addition to the requirement to love others, lends a crucial dimension to "love" as a theological virtue: we love God because he first loved us (1 John 4:19), and we are to love others as we love ourselves (Matt. 22:39). In reference to Aristotle's *Nicomachean Ethics*, Thomas Aquinas held that love of others presupposes love of self—these two loves are complementary, construed as a single love. One cannot properly love one's neighbor if one lacks self-love. It is in love for others that love of self finds fulfillment.[111] Recall the opening statement in Adam Smith's first great work: that concern for neighbor is crucial to self-interest.[112] The supremacy of love in the faith-hope-love theological triad is the key to Scripture's emphasis on human flourishing, since without love there can be no

110. 1 Cor. 13.

111. See *Summa theologiae*, *Summa contra gentiles*, and *Scriptum super libros sententiarum*, by Thomas Aquinas, cited in van Vliet, "Ontology of Human Flourishing," 250.

112. *TMS*, 9.

concern for the poor. Humanity is predisposed to seek the welfare of fellow humanity. "If I give away all I have . . . but have not love, I gain nothing. . . . Love . . . believes all things, hopes all things. . . . So now faith, hope, and love abide, these three; but the greatest of these is love" (1 Cor. 13:3, 7, 13).

Secondly, faith is to believe what one does not see. Its reward is to see what is believed. Thus, faith, oriented to the present as it is, also has an intertemporal dimension, conveying the notion of trust and conviction in, typically, a metaphysical reality. One who has faith cannot mistrust.

Finally, hope also represents our firm, optimistic, and patient waiting for these promises to unfold in the future. Hope, therefore, is also intertemporal: it is future-looking. One who has hope cannot be dissuaded. While faith goes before, hope follows after.[113]

### Human Flourishing: The Eschatological Reality—Living in Hope

The virtues of both faith and hope demonstrate humanity's existential location—its eschatological reality—as inhabiting both the already and the not yet:

> Women and men live in the present, exercising faith in the reality of living on this side of the cross and resurrection. Hope, on the other hand, locates us in the "not yet" of the parousia —the consummation of the kingdom at the return of Christ. The kingdom of God (or "heaven") belongs to the age to come; the present age will never realize all that the kingdom of God means, for it is marred and inhabited by evil and a deeply flawed humanity upon whom the image of God continues to reside, if in deeply muted form. Perfected human flourishing in the consummated kingdom is the hope of humanity, and it is in

113. van Vliet, "Ontology of Human Flourishing," 249.

> faith and hope that humans live in a world broken by pain and suffering and the perpetration of unspeakable evil.[114]

Unmistakably echoing the already–not yet eschatological framework of Bob Goudzwaard in citing Dietrich Bonhoeffer, that "we should be living from the meaning coming to us from the end," N. T. Wright maintains that the redemption of all creation —a three-dimensional renewal of space, time, and matter— focuses on justice, beauty, and evangelism. The term "justice" he uses "as a shorthand for the intention of God, expressed from Genesis to Revelation, to set the whole world right—a plan gloriously fulfilled in Jesus Christ."[115] Doing justice in the world is part of the Christian task; it is within the design of humanity's general hope and a part of the task of renewal facing the Christian inhabiting an inaugurated eschatology. This is the new cosmology of the post-Easter world. "Justice," for Wright, means righting the wrongs inherent in globalization, manifested in the chasm between the rich and the poor.[116] This will bring about human flourishing, a task reaching completion and perfection with Jesus' return, but a task that human beings, as image bearers of God and thus capable of creating beauty, have an extraordinary ability to be part of.[117] Adam Smith, Bob Goudzwaard, and N. T. Wright all exhibit a similar view of justice in an ideal world of

114. van Vliet, "Ontology of Human Flourishing," 250.

115. N. T. Wright, *Surprised by Hope: Rethinking Heaven, the Resurrection, and the Mission of the Church* (New York: HarperCollins, 2008), 213–16.

116. van Vliet, "Ontology of Human Flourishing," 251–52, and Wright, *Surprised by Hope*, 216–22. Notice that both Bob Goudzwaard and N. T. Wright have similar emphases on the crippling impact on human flourishing brought about by globalization.

117. Wright, *Surprised by Hope*, 223. Compare Wright's emphasis on the human capacity to create beauty with the prominence given to it by Abraham Kuyper in his *Wisdom and Wonder: Common Grace in Science and Art* (Grand Rapids: Christian's Library Press, 2011), reviewed in my "Abraham Kuyper's Wisdom and Wonder: Review Essay," *Pro Rege* 41, no. 1 (2012): 16–23, at https://digitalcollections.dordt.edu/pro_rege/vol41/iss1/3.

human well-being and flourishing, while the obvious difference, of course, is Adam Smith's lack of grounding in the eschatological reality of Christian theism.

Over eight billion people, each one created in the image of God, populate the earth. Despite sometimes vastly differing religious commitments among these people, that created humanity shares a common agape love, to a greater or lesser degree, for fellow men and women. It is this that drives the habits of the heart to yearn and work, even now, and in a spirit of hope, toward a consummated future of human prosperity and flourishing. But only the Reformed Christian can look forward to such a consummation with hope and confidence. Adam Smith's social philosophy and political economy represent wonderful and commendable social goals and economic structures toward which to work, but only the moral and theological commitments of Christian theism can deliver such a world with ultimate absolute certainty in lives self-consciously lived *coram deo*.

# 5

# CONCLUDING REMARKS

The scholarly imperative driving this volume has been to ascertain the *status quaestionis* of Adam Smith studies, to explicate its analytical content, and to determine its value in the life and thought of the Reformed Christian. In navigating the contours of this vast and sometimes complex landscape, our focus has necessarily been on Smith's works on moral philosophy and political economy, which together constitute his *magna opera*. The curated themes and subthemes presented in the foregoing study have underscored the common line of development of *TMS* and *WN*, a continuity that was finally understood two centuries after their composition. The narrative arc throughout these two works is the construction of a flourishing society peopled by men and women of virtue who subscribe to a high ethical code. This culture advances materially by means of a political economy that treasures morality, freedom, and liberty. While happiness (or welfare) is defined in philosophical terms in *TMS* as "our ability to act according to the rules of positive morality," *WN* focuses on welfare in material terms (the level of real income). This is not a contradiction in Smith's thought; rather, it demonstrates the consideration of two areas of human experience.

The corruption of moral sentiments (*TMS*) would invariably result in an unbridled pursuit of gain (*WN*).

Moreover, our study has shown that much contemporary understanding of Adam Smith and his work is wrongheaded and misguided due to partial or poor reading of him. We see this particularly in the tired populist tropes of, to name just a few: antigovernment sentiment, "economic man" (*homo economicus*), and laissez-faire economics, many of these being contrivances that postdated Adam Smith, but all of them representing conceptual categories and labels that were entirely foreign to Adam Smith and which he would have strongly opposed. Adam Smith caught the ethos and addressed the needs of his own day, but, more than that, his work is of enduring relevance today, where virtue ethics as a commonly understood and shared paradigm for life in society has disappeared. It has been replaced by a social philosophy centered on the idolatry of consumerism. Limitless acquisition of material goods has replaced faith in God as the guarantor of our ultimate security, safety, and meaning. Love of money has become the end of all things; its pursuit has displaced the kingdom of God as our ultimate *summum bonum*. And for this Adam Smith is blamed by those poorly informed and clamorous misinterpreters mentioned above.

Far from prescribing a "dog eat dog" political economy, Smith always sided with the poor and underprivileged. He despised the greed of merchants—particularly their attempts to curry favor with the government in order to enlarge their already outsized entrenched privilege. While he prescribed the sweeping away of controls and restrictions on economic activity, he had nothing but scorn for monopolies and charged government with the responsibility to censure all forms of economic activity that gave power to the managers and "capitalists," a label he never used. Instead, Smith used the phrases "liberal plan" or "system of natural liberty." But make no mistake, for Smith liberty is not limitless: it must serve the common good and further universal benevolence. Such liberty reinforces trade on a personal and national level, the propelling heart of free market economics. Human flourishing depends on just such trade and the innate human desire to improve. Such a market system has a limited role for government, but an essential role nonetheless. While government has no economic function in Smith's prescription of political economy, free markets can only function with the observance of rules.

Adam Smith's moral philosophy and political economy have great relevance for our crumbling twenty-first-century society, where little attention is paid to an ethical system based on virtue and justice, replaced by a relativism that is incapable of recognizing the true, the good, and the beautiful, and a deeply fractured economic system driven by vested interests and characterized by a chasm between the rich and the poor. Consequently, there is much fodder in Smith's *magna opera* to be harvested and employed by Christian theists in their endeavors to restore a moral and material world, characterized by human flourishing with the necessary preconditions of moral and economic rectitude. Yes, Adam Smith's personal metaphysic and antifoundationalism explain his socially constructed rules for morality. Moreover, his social imaginary and religion place him at odds with that of the Christian theist and forecloses any interpretation locating him unambiguously in the Reformed Christian camp. Yet, as has been demonstrated, his seminal contributions to the fields of moral philosophy and political economy speak directly to our contemporaneous reality. The resultant prescriptions for a flourishing and virtuous society, and the commitment to the well-being of humankind found in his *magna opera*, should resonate with all humanity and have particular value for the Reformed Christian today in the recovery of kingdom shalom.

# GLOSSARY

**belles lettres**. French for "beautiful letters." Works of literature that are artistically beautiful and pleasing, being more imaginative than technical and scientific writings, are considered belles lettres.

**capital deepening**. An increase in the capital-labor ratio. The capital-labor ratio can go higher either due to an increase in the capital stock or through a decrease in the number of workers. Capital deepening increases the marginal product of labor—i.e., it makes labor more productive (because there are now more units of capital per worker). Capital deepening improves the productivity of labor, a central teaching of *WN*.

**capitalism**. An economic system characterized by private ownership and initiative. Basic to such a system is private property, the right of ownership, and the use of wealth to earn income. Also called *free enterprise system*.

**casuistry**. A resolving of specific cases of conscience, duty, or conduct through interpretation of ethical principles or religious doctrine.

**classical economics**. An economic theory holding that a self-regulating economy is the most efficient and successful because individuals adjust to meet one another's demands as these arise. According to classical economic theory, government intervention is unnecessary, since the economy's citizens will efficiently distribute scarce resources to suit individuals' and enterprises' needs. Adam Smith is regarded as the father of classical economics. Compare **neoclassical economics**.

**commercial society**. A social group constituted by a set of principles, or mechanisms, the two most important of which are moral sentiments and competitive markets.

**contingence**. A state of dependency of persons, events, and things on other persons, events, and things. The Christian God is noncontingent and self-contained. Humanity and its existence are contingent and dependent.

**deism**. Belief in the existence of a supreme being, specifically of a creator who does not intervene in the universe. The term is used chiefly of an intellectual movement of the seventeenth and eighteenth centuries that accepted the existence of a creator on the basis of reason, but rejected belief in a supernatural deity who interacts with humankind.

**double coincidence of wants**. The situation that arises when each party in an **exchange economy** happens to have what the other party desires. The introduction of money as a means of exchange abolishes the need to meet this nearly impossible situation.

**economics**. The study of the allocation of scarce resources among competing uses, employing statistical methods and mathematical modeling to explain markets and the behavior of households, businesses, industries, and governments. See **classical economics**, **macroeconomics**, **microeconomics**, **neoclassical economics**, **physiocracy**.

**exchange economy**. A rudimentary economy in which an economic agent is the subject of exchange and the good is the object of exchange. Each agent brings his or her own endowment, and they can exchange products. Compare **political economy**.

**jurisprudence**. The science or philosophy of law dealing with the principles of positive law and legal relations. It is a formal or analytical science, rather than a material one.

**macroeconomics**. The study of the economy of an entire nation or society, focusing on the composite categories of national output, employment, and price levels. Compare **microeconomics**.

**mercantilism**. An economic policy, pursued by nearly all the trading nations in the seventeenth and early eighteenth centuries, that seeks to increase a nation's wealth and power by encouraging the export of goods in return for gold. This policy necessitates high degrees of involvement by government through the enactment of practices favoring domestic merchants, such as the erection of tariff barriers and the subsidizing of domestic competing industries.

**metaphysics**. A division of philosophy that is concerned with the fundamental nature of reality and being. This includes ontology (existence and being), cosmology (the nature of the universe), and often epistemology (theory of knowledge, its source, and its limit).

**microeconomics**. The study of the economy that focuses on the behavior of economic agents—people (households), businesses, government, and the financial system—each category of which is in pursuit of maximizing its particular economic objective in the market. Compare **macroeconomics**.

**neoclassical economics**. An analytical approach to the study of economics that uses supply and demand to describe the production, pricing, consumption, and distribution of products and services. It combines **classical economics**' cost-of-production theory with the concepts of utility maximization. Stanley Jevons, Maria Edgeworth, Leon Walras, Vilfredo Pareto, and other economists contributed to the development of neoclassical economics. John Stuart Mill, commonly located in the classical camp, began the movement to neoclassicism.

**phenomenology**. Our moral judgments' being normative through the way in which we actually make them, apart from any foundational theory or set of general principles. Our moral justification and moral critique are immanent to, not transcendent of, our moral practice and, as such, are highly relativistic because we are deeply shaped by our local societies in the way in which we make moral judgments.

**physiocracy**. An eighteenth-century school of **economics** maintaining that land was the single source of income and wealth, and that this "natural order" should remain entirely free from government interference. The principle of laissez-faire developed from this philosophy.

**political economy**. The study of the relationships between individuals and society and between markets and the state. The term is derived from the Greek *polis,* meaning "city" or "state," and from *oikonomos,* meaning "one who manages a household or estate." Political economy thus addresses the management of a country—the public's household—accounting for social, political, historical, and economic factors. The historical formation of political economy long predated social science as a discipline, being typically located within the discipline of philosophy. Compare **exchange economy**.

**polymath**. A person of wide-ranging knowledge and learning, typically spanning multiple, often unrelated, disciplines.

**reification**. The taking of an abstract idea and making it concrete; the giving of definite content and form to a concept or idea.

**social imaginary**. The common understanding and expectations people have about life in society. A social imaginary fosters a sense of legitimacy and shared identity that give a society coherence. It is more often passed on via the stories, traditions, and rituals of a society than expressed in explicit or theoretical terms.

***status quaestionis***. Latin for, roughly, "the state of investigation." The term is most commonly employed in scholarly literature to refer in a summary way to the accumulated results, scholarly consensus, and areas remaining to be developed on any given topic.

**Stoicism**. An ancient philosophy of the Hellenistic period (323 to 31 B.C.). It teaches that philosophy is a way of living a virtuous life. The primacy of self-control is intrinsic to Stoic philosophy. Following Marcus Aurelius, Adam Smith highly esteemed and admired the virtue of self-control. They both believed in an impartial, self-scrutinizing conscience that guided morality; while Aurelius called it the *God within*, Smith called it the *impartial spectator*.

# BIBLIOGRAPHY


Ames, William. *Conscience with the Power and Cases Thereof. Devided into V. Bookes*. 1639. Reprint, Norwood, NJ: Walter J. Johnson, 1975.

Aspromourgos, Tony. "Adam Smith on Labour and Capital." In *The Oxford Handbook of Adam Smith,* edited by Christopher J. Berry, Maria Pia Paganelli, and Craig Smith, 267–89. Oxford: Oxford University Press, 2013.

Banerjee, Abhijit V., and Esther Duflo. *Poor Economics: A Radical Rethinking of the Way to Fight Global Poverty*. New York: Public Affairs, 2012.

Berkhof, Louis. *Systematic Theology*. 4th ed. Grand Rapids: Eerdmans, 1941.

Berry, Christopher J. "Adam Smith: An Outline of Life, Times, and Legacy." In *The Oxford Handbook of Adam Smith,* edited by Christopher J. Berry, Maria Pia Paganelli, and Craig Smith, 1–20. Oxford: Oxford University Press, 2013.

Berry, Christopher J., Maria Pia Paganelli, and Craig Smith, eds. *The Oxford Handbook of Adam Smith*. Oxford: Oxford University Press, 2013.

Broadie, Alexander. "Sympathy and the Impartial Spectator." In *The Cambridge Companion to Adam Smith,* edited by Knud Haakonssen, 158–88. Cambridge: Cambridge University Press, 2006.

Brue, Stanley L., and Randy R. Grant, eds. *The Evolution of Economic Thought.* 8th ed. Mason, OH: South-Western, 2013.

Buchan, James. "The Biography of Adam Smith." In *Adam Smith: His Life, Thought, and Legacy,* edited by Ryan Patrick Hanley, 3–16. Princeton, NJ: Princeton University Press, 2016.

Butler, Eamonn. *The Condensed Wealth of Nations and the Incredibly Condensed Theory of Moral Sentiments.* [London:] Adam Smith Institute, 2011.

Calvin, John. *Institutes of the Christian Religion.* Edited by John T. McNeill. Translated by Ford Lewis Battles. Philadelphia: Westminster Press, 1960.

Campbell, R. H., and A. S. Skinner. "General Introduction." In *An Inquiry into the Nature and Causes of the Wealth of Nations.* Edited by R. H. Campbell, A. S. Skinner, and W. B. Todd, 1-60. 2 vols. Oxford: Oxford University Press, 1976. First published 1776. 1–60.

Chambers, Robert, and Thomas Napier Thomson. *A Biographical Dictionary of Eminent Scotsmen.* Glasgow: Blackie and Son, 1857.

*The Confession of Faith, the Larger and Shorter Catechisms, with the Scripture Proofs at Large.* Glasgow: Free Presbyterian Publications, 1994.

"The Defining Characteristics of a Good and Faithful Steward." *Biblical Stewardship,* February 23, 2018. https://www.taylor.edu/news/the-defining-characteristics-of-a-good-and-faithful-steward#:~:text=The%20good%20and%20faithful%20steward,of%20how%20subtle%20or%20how.

Dooyeweerd, Herman. *A New Critique of Theoretical Thought.* Translated by David H. Freeman and William S. Young.

4 vols. Philadelphia: Presbyterian and Reformed, 1953–58. Originally published as *De Wijsbegeerte der Wetsidee*. 3 vols. Amsterdam: H. J. Paris, 1935–36.

Duncan, Ligon. "Berkhof on the Nature of the Biblical Concept of Covenant." July 14, 2019. https://ligonduncan.com/berkhof-on-the-nature-of-the-biblical-concept-of-covenant/.

Easterly, William R. *The Elusive Quest for Growth: Economists' Adventures and Misadventures in the Tropics*. Cambridge, MA: MIT Press, 2001.

———. *The Tyranny of Experts: Economists, Dictators, and the Forgotten Rights of the Poor*. New York: Basic Books, 2014.

———. *The White Man's Burden: Why the West's Efforts to Aid the Rest Have Done So Much Ill and So Little Good*. New York: Penguin, 2006.

Erickson, Millard J. *Christian Theology*. 2nd ed. Grand Rapids: Baker Academic, 2002.

Evensky, Jerry. "The Wealth of Nations." In *Adam Smith: His Life, Thought, and Legacy*, edited by Ryan Patrick Hanley, 67–88. Princeton, NJ: Princeton University Press, 2016.

Fleischacker, Samuel. "Adam Smith's Moral and Political Philosophy." In *Stanford Encyclopedia of Philosophy*. November 11, 2020. https://plato.stanford.edu/entries/smith-moral-political/#SumSmiMor.

———. *On Adam Smith's* Wealth of Nations*: A Philosophical Companion*. Princeton, NJ: Princeton University Press, 2005.

Frame, John. *The Doctrine of God*. Phillipsburg, NJ: P&R Publishing, 2002.

Fricke, Christel. "Adam Smith: The Sympathetic Process and the Origin and Function of Conscience." In *The Oxford Handbook of Adam Smith*, edited by Christopher J. Berry, Maria Pia Paganelli, and Craig Smith, 176–200. Oxford: Oxford University Press, 2013.

Furniss, Edgar S. *The Position of the Laborer in a System of Nationalism*. Boston: Houghton Mifflin, 1920.

Galbraith, John Kenneth. *The Culture of Contentment*. Boston: Houghton Mifflin, 1992.

Gill, Michael B. "Lord Shaftesbury [Anthony Ashley Cooper, 3rd Earl of Shaftesbury]." In *Stanford Encyclopedia of Philosophy Archive*. Winter 2017 Edition. https://plato.stanford.edu/archives/win2017/entries/shaftesbury/.

Goudzwaard, Bob. *Aid for the Overdeveloped West*. Toronto, ON: Wedge Publishing, 1975.

———. *Capitalism and Progress: A Diagnosis of Western Society*. Translated and edited by Josina van Nuis Zylstra. Toronto, ON: Wedge Publishing, 1979.

———. *Globalization and the Kingdom of God*. Responses by Brian Fikkert, Larry Reed, and Adolfo Garcia de la Sienra. Edited by James W. Skillen. Grand Rapids: Baker Books, 2001.

———. *Idols of Our Time*. Translated by Mark Vander Vennen. Downers Grove, IL: InterVarsity Press, 1984.

Goudzwaard, Bob, and Harry de Lange. *Beyond Poverty and Affluence: Toward an Economy of Care with a Twelve-Step Program for Economic Recovery*. Translated and edited by Mark R. Vander Vennen. Grand Rapids: Eerdmans, 1995.

Graham, Gordon. "Adam Smith and Religion." In *Adam Smith: His Life, Thought, and Legacy*, edited by Ryan Patrick Hanley, 305–20. Princeton, NJ: Princeton University Press, 2016.

Griswold, Charles L., Jr. *Adam Smith and the Virtues of Enlightenment*. Cambridge: Cambridge University Press, 1999.

Haakonssen, Knud, ed. *The Cambridge Companion to Adam Smith*. Cambridge: Cambridge University Press, 2006.

———. "Introduction: The Coherence of Smith's Thought." In *The Cambridge Companion to Adam Smith*, edited by Knud Haakonssen, 1–21. Cambridge: Cambridge University Press, 2006.

———. "Smith, Adam (1763–90)." In *The Routledge Encyclopedia of Philosophy*, edited by E. Craig, 1:815–22. London: Routledge, 1998.

Hanley, Ryan Patrick. *Adam Smith and the Character of Virtue*. New York: Cambridge University Press, 2009.

———, ed. *Adam Smith: His Life, Thought, and Legacy*. Princeton, NJ: Princeton University Press, 2016.

———. "Bringing Religion Back In: Remarks on Gordon Graham." *Journal of Scottish Philosophy* 17, no. 1 (2019): 6–12.

"Hard Work and Black Swans." *The Economist*, September 5, 2020.

Heilbroner, Robert L. "Adam Smith: Scottish Philosopher." March 7, 2024. https://www.britannica.com/biography/Adam-Smith.

Herdt, Jennifer A. "Calvin's Legacy for Contemporary Reformed Natural Law." *Scottish Journal of Theology* 67, no. 4 (2014): 414–35.

Jonsson, Fredrik Albritton. "Adam Smith and Enlightenment Studies." In *Adam Smith: His Life, Thought, and Legacy*, edited by Ryan Patrick Hanley, 443–58. Princeton, NJ: Princeton University Press, 2016.

Kennedy, Gavin. "Adam Smith: Some Popular Uses and Abuses." In *Adam Smith: His Life, Thought, and Legacy*, edited by Ryan Patrick Hanley, 461–77. Princeton, NJ: Princeton University Press, 2016.

———. *An Authentic Account of Adam Smith*. Cham, Switzerland: Palgrave Macmillan, 2017.

Keynes, John Maynard. *The End of Laissez-Faire*. London: Hogarth, 1926.

Koebner, Richard. "Adam Smith and the Industrial Revolution." *The Economic History Review* 11, no. 3 (1959): 381–91.

Kurz, Heinz D. *Economic Thought: A Brief History*. Translated by Jeremiah Riemer. New York: Columbia University Press, 2016.

Kuyper, Abraham. "Manual Labor." Edited by Harry Van Dyke. Translated by Reinder Bruinsma. In *On Business and*

*Economics*, edited by Peter S. Heslam, 145–68. Bellingham, WA: Lexham, 2021.

———. "Meditations." Translated by Harry Van Dyke. In *On Business and Economics*, edited by Peter S. Heslam, 355–86. Bellingham, WA: Lexham, 2021.

———. *On Business and Economics*. Edited by Peter S. Heslam. Bellingham, WA: Lexham, 2021.

———. *On Charity and Justice*. Edited by Matthew J. Tuininga. Bellingham, WA: Lexham, 2022.

———. *Our Program: A Christian Political Manifesto*. Translated and edited by Harry Van Dyke. Bellingham, WA: Lexham, 2015.

———. "The Sacred Order." Translated by Harry Van Dyke. In *On Business and Economics*, edited by Peter S. Heslam, 313–16. Bellingham, WA: Lexham, 2021.

———. "The Social Question and the Christian Religion." Translated by Harry Van Dyke. In *On Business and Economics*, edited by Peter S. Heslam, 171–229. Bellingham, WA: Lexham, 2021.

———. *Wisdom and Wonder: Common Grace in Science and Art*. Grand Rapids: Christian's Library Press, 2011.

LaHaye, Laura. "Mercantilism." https://www.econlib.org/library/Enc/Mercantilism.html.

"*Laissez-faire*." In Wikipedia. https://en.wikipedia.org/wiki/Laissez-faire.

Lems, Shane. "The Bible and Foundationalism." May 12, 2009. https://reformedreader.wordpress.com/2009/05/12/the-bible-and-foundationalism/.

Lieberman, David. "Adam Smith on Justice, Rights, and Law." In *The Cambridge Companion to Adam Smith*, edited by Knud Haakonssen, 214–45. Cambridge: Cambridge University Press, 2006.

London, C. W. "What Was Mercantilism?" *The Economist*, August 23, 2013. https://www.economist.com/free-exchange/2013/08/23/what-was-mercantilism.

MacGregor, D. H. *Economic Thought and Policy*. Oxford: Oxford University Press, 1949.

MacIntyre, Alasdair. *Whose Justice? Which Rationality?* South Bend, IN: University of Notre Dame Press, 1988.

Mandeville, Bernard. *Fable of the Bees*. Edited by F. B. Kaye. London: Oxford University Press, 1924.

Mill, John Stuart. *Essays on Some Unsettled Questions of Political Economy*. 2nd ed. London: Longmans, Green, Reader & Dyer, 1874.

———. "On the Definition of Political Economy, and on the Method of Investigation Proper to It." *London and Westminster Review*, October 1836.

Muller, Jerry Z. *Adam Smith in His Time and Ours: Designing the Decent Society*. Princeton, NJ: Princeton University Press, 1995.

Murray, John. *Principles of Conduct: Aspects of Biblical Ethics*. Grand Rapids: Eerdmans, 1957.

Norman, Jesse. "Why David Hume and Adam Smith Were the Original Odd Couple: The Engines of the Enlightenment." *Prospect*, September 2017.

Paganelli, Maria Pia. "Adam Smith and Economic Development in Theory and Practice: A Rejection of the Stadial Model?" *Journal of the History of Economic Thought* 44, no. 1 (March 2022): 95–104.

———. "Adam Smith and the History of Economic Thought: The Case of Banking." In *Adam Smith: His Life, Thought, and Legacy*, edited by Ryan Patrick Hanley, 247–61. Princeton, NJ: Princeton University Press, 2016.

Peil, Jan, and Irene van Staveren. *Handbook of Economics and Ethics*. Cheltenham, UK: Edward Elgar, 2009.

Phillipson, Nicholas. "Adam Smith: A Biographer's Reflection." In *The Oxford Handbook of Adam Smith*, edited by Christopher J. Berry, Maria Pia Paganelli, and Craig Smith, 23–35. Oxford: Oxford University Press, 2013.

Rae, John. *Life of Adam Smith*. London: Macmillan, 1895.

Raphael, D. D., and A. L. Macfie. "Introduction." In *The Theory of Moral Sentiments*, by Adam Smith. Indianapolis, IN: Liberty Fund, 1982.

Rasmussen, Dennis. *The Problems and Promise of Commercial Society: Adam Smith's Response to Rousseau*. University Park, PA: Pennsylvania State University Press, 2008.

Ravallion, Martin. *The Economics of Poverty: History, Measurement, and Policy*. New York: Oxford University Press, 2016. Accompanied by his website at https://economicsandpoverty.com.

Ross, Ian Simpson. *The Life of Adam Smith*. Oxford: Oxford University Press, 1995.

Sachs, Jeffrey D. *Common Wealth: Economics for a Crowded Planet*. New York: Penguin, 2008.

———. *The End of Poverty: Economic Possibilities for Our Time*. New York: Penguin, 2005.

Schliesser, Eric. "The Theory of Moral Sentiments." In *Adam Smith: His Life, Thought, and Legacy*, edited by Ryan Patrick Hanley, 33–47. Princeton, NJ: Princeton University Press, 2016.

Scoles, Henry C. "Stewardship, Efficiency and Effectiveness." July 3, 2018. https://www.linkedin.com/pulse/stewardship-efficiency-effectiveness-henry-scoles/.

Scott, William R. "The Never to Be Forgotten Hutcheson: Excerpts from W. R. Scott." *Economic Journal Watch* 8, no. 1 (2011): 96–109.

Sen, Amartya. "Adam Smith and Economic Development." In *Adam Smith: His Life, Thought, and Legacy*, edited by Ryan Patrick Hanley, 281–302. Princeton, NJ: Princeton University Press, 2016.

———. *Development as Freedom*. Oxford: Oxford University Press, 1999.

———. *The Idea of Justice*. Cambridge, MA: Harvard University Press, 2009.

———. *On Economic Inequality*. Oxford: Oxford University Press, 1973.

———. "Uses and Abuses of Adam Smith." *History of Political Economy* 43 (2011): 257–71.

Skinner, Andrew. "Introduction." In *The Wealth of Nations, Books I-III*, by Adam Smith, edited by Skinner, 11–97. New York: Penguin Books, 1979.

Smith, Adam. *The Correspondence of Adam Smith*. Edited by Ernest Campbell Mossner and Ian Simpson Ross. Oxford: Oxford University Press, 1977. 2nd ed. 1987.

———. *Essays on Philosophical Subjects*. Edited by W. P. D. Wightman, J. C. Bryce, and Ian Simpson Ross. Oxford: Oxford University Press, 1980. First published posthumously in 1795.

———. *An Inquiry into the Nature and Causes of the Wealth of Nations*. Edited by R. H. Campbell, A. S. Skinner, and W. B. Todd. 2 vols. Oxford: Oxford University Press, 1976. First published 1776.

———. *Lectures on Jurisprudence*. Edited by Ronald L. Meek, D. D. Raphael, and Peter G. Stein. Oxford: Oxford University Press, 1978. Includes *LJ(A)* (1762–63) and *LJ(B)* (1766). Unpublished in the author's lifetime.

———. *Lectures on Rhetoric and Belles Lettres*. Edited by J. C. Bryce and Andrew S. Skinner. Oxford: Oxford University Press, 1983. Unpublished in the author's lifetime.

———. *The Theory of Moral Sentiments*. Edited by D. D. Raphael and A. L. MacFie. Oxford: Oxford University Press, 1976. First published 1759–90.

Smith, Eugene. "Adam Smith and Self-Interest." In *The Oxford Handbook of Adam Smith*, edited by Christopher J. Berry, Maria Pia Paganelli, and Craig Smith, 241–64. Oxford: Oxford University Press, 2013.

Sproul, R. C. "What Is Biblical Stewardship?" 2016. Reprint, September 29, 2023. https://www.ligonier.org/learn/articles/what-biblical-stewardship.

Stewart, Dugald. "Account of the Life and Writings of Adam Smith, LL.D." (1793). In *EPS*, 269–351.

van den Heuvel, Steven C., ed. *Historical and Multidisciplinary Perspectives on Hope*. Cham, Switzerland: Springer, 2020.

Van Til, Cornelius. *Christian Theistic Ethics*. Phillipsburg, NJ: Presbyterian and Reformed, 1980.

———. *The Defense of the Faith*. 3rd ed. Phillipsburg, NJ: Presbyterian and Reformed, 1967.

van Vliet, Jan. "Abraham Kuyper's Wisdom and Wonder: Review Essay." *Pro Rege* 41, no. 1 (2012): 16–23.

———. "An Ontology of Human Flourishing: Economic Development and Epistemologies of Faith, Hope, and Love." In *Historical and Multidisciplinary Perspectives on Hope*, edited by Steven C. van den Heuvel, 239–61. Cham, Switzerland: Springer, 2020.

———. *The Rise of Reformed System: The Intellectual Heritage of William Ames*. Eugene, OR: Wipf & Stock, 2013.

Vandenberg, Phyllis. "Bernard Mandeville (1670–1733)." *Internet Encyclopedia of Philosophy*. https://iep.utm.edu/mandevil/.

Vandenberg, Phyllis, and Abigail DeHart. "Francis Hutcheson (1694–1745)." *Internet Encyclopedia of Philosophy*. https://iep.utm.edu/hutcheso/.

Vlot, Adrian, and Bob Goudzwaard. "We Are People of the Way: An Impression of the Final Session of the Conference." *Philosophia Reformata* 66, no. 1 (2001): 142–52

Vos, Geerhardus. *The Teaching of Jesus concerning the Kingdom of God and the Church*. New York: American Tract Society, 1903.

Weinstein, Jack Russell. "Adam Smith (1723–90)." *Internet Encyclopedia of Philosophy*. https://iep.utm.edu/smith/.

Whatmore, Richard. "Adam Smith's Role in the French Revolution." *Past and Present* 175 (May 2002): 65–89.

Wilson, David, and William Dixon. *A History of Homo Economicus: The Nature of the Moral in Economic Theory*. London: Routledge, 2012.

Wodehouse, P. G. *The Clicking of Cuthbert*. 1922. Reprint, Woodstock: Overlook Press, 2002.

Wolfe, Samuel T. *A Key to Dooyeweerd*. Nutley, NJ: Presbyterian and Reformed, 1977.

Wolterstorff, Nicholas. "Adam Smith on Justice and Injustice." In *Adam Smith: His Life, Thought, and Legacy*, edited by Ryan Patrick Hanley, 173–91. Princeton, NJ: Princeton University Press, 2016.

———. *Justice: Rights and Wrongs*. Princeton, NJ: Princeton University Press: 2008.

Wright, N. T. *Surprised by Hope: Rethinking Heaven, the Resurrection, and the Mission of the Church*. New York: HarperCollins, 2008.

Young, Jeffrey T. "Andrew Skinner, the Glasgow Edition, and Adam Smith." *Œconomia* 2–3 (2012): 365–76.

# INDEX OF SUBJECTS AND NAMES

**Jan van Vliet** (PhD, Westminster Theological Seminary) is emeritus professor of economics at Dordt University, Sioux Center, Iowa. He holds advanced degrees in both economics and theological studies from Canada and the United States and has spent many years working in these disciplines in both countries. He is a member of, among others, the *Evangelical Theological Society* and the *Society for Reformation Research*, and past member of the *Kuyper Translation Society* that produced the *Abraham Kuyper Collected Works in Public Theology* (2017).

His areas of interest and scholarly competencies include Reformation and post-Reformation theology, philosophy, and ethics, while his interests in economics include philosophical economics, shifting economic paradigms, and poverty alleviation with special reference to Kuyperian public theology and Reformational social philosophy. He has taught, among other places, at the University of Toronto (economics) and Prairie College (Three Hills, Alberta—theology).

His other books are *The Rise of Reformed System: The Intellectual Heritage of William Ames* (2013), and he was the translator of Abraham Kuyper's *Om de Oudewereld Zee* (2 vols. 1907–8) which appeared as *On Islam* (2017). He has spoken at conferences in Canada, the United States, and Europe.

Van Vliet is on the board of Soccer Chaplains United (https://soccerchaplainsunited.org/) and on the Editorial Advisory Board of *Neocalviniana* (https://neocalviniana.org/). He lives with his wife in Sioux Center, Iowa.